Lifemaps of People
with Learning Difficulties

Lifemaps of People
with Learning Difficulties

Barry Gray and Geoff Ridden

Jessica Kingsley Publishers
London and Philadelphia

The right of Barry Gray and Geoff Ridden to be identified as authors of this work has been asserted by them in accordance with the Copyright, Designs and Patents Act 1988.

First published in the United Kingdom in 1999 by
Jessica Kingsley Publishers Ltd,
116 Pentonville Road, London
N1 9JB, England
and
325 Chestnut Street,
Philadelphia PA 19106, USA.

www.jkp.com

Original artwork provided by the students and subjects of the stories in this book.

© Copyright 1999 Barry Gray and Geoff Ridden

Library of Congress Cataloging in Publication Data
Gray, Barry, 1944–
Lifemaps of people with learning disabilities / Barry Gray and Geoff Ridden.
p.   cm.   Includes bibliographical references and index.
ISBN 1 85302 690 5 (alk. paper)
1. Social work with the mentally handicapped--Psychological aspects.
2. Mentally handicapped--Biography. 3. Mentally handicapped--Psychology.
4. Learning disabled--Biography. 5. Learning disabled--Psychology.
6. Psychology--Biographical methods. I. Ridden, G.M. II. Title.
HV3004.G73   1999   362.3'092'2--dc21

British Library Cataloguing in Publication Data
Gray, Barry
Lifemaps of people with learning disabilities
1. Learning disabled 2. Learning disabled – Biography
I. Title II. Ridden, Geoff
362.3

ISBN 1 85302 690 5

Printed and Bound in Great Britain by
Athenaeum Press, Gateshead, Tyne and Wear

Contents

Acknowledgements

First, we wish to express our thanks to the people who allowed us to tell their life stories and to those who collected them: Megan Arden, Melanie Andrews, Nigel Biggs, Joanna Brown, Dominie Burton, Jennifer Harkness, Matthew Horne, Paul Kniveton, Sophie Kniveton, Lucy O'Flanagan, Karen Patterson, Yoko Watts and Wendy Wilcocks. Thanks also to Karen Trevithick for her help in drafting, at very short notice, and to Peter Dixon, for the poem on page 7.

We are especially grateful for the help of our families and friends in supporting this project and in adding comments and suggestions through many conversations about it.

Billy was super at telly
And knew every programme there was.
He was super at helping to tidy
                    and cleaning
                    and finding
                    and jobs.

He was bestest at guessing and laughing.
At sorting, and putting away.
And sharing his crisps,
And his peanuts,
Inventing new games we could play.
He was smashing at jokes and at acting
Unknotting laces,
And games
He knew every face
In the Infants'
And called everyone by their names,
                    Penny
                    Peter
                    Paul
                    and James

    Billy shared in all their games.
    He always gave way in a squabble.
    At teasing he never got wild –
    But TESTERS said Billy was useless
    And called him –
        A Less Able Child.

Peter Dixon

1

Introduction

Life stories and the construction of identity

From the briefest of written descriptions of people, how much do we infer about their personality, their status, their behaviour? And how biased and misleading can such descriptions be?

In the case of people with learning disabilities, there is a real danger that certain factors which, in the case of most people, play a key role in the determination of identity, become ignored. Gender, age, ethnicity, religious persuasion, sexual orientation and even the possession of money all are overlooked, and the only determinant of identity of any strength or power is the label 'disability'.

One of the contributors to this collection identifies a real difficulty in coming to terms with the personality and individual identity of a man with learning difficulties:

> I was ... given access to his case notes by the manager of the home, which contained very factual, impersonal information about Tim, which did not, really, reflect his life history. There were a great number of gaps in the case file, with many unexplained details of his whereabouts. (p.70)

There is a real danger that any sense of the identity of a person with learning difficulties is subsumed beneath a prevailing desire to label, to pigeon-hole, to file and thereby to control.

Much work has been done in Cultural Studies this decade to investigate the factors which construct identity and those factors which are suppressed in the construction of the identity of marginalised groups. In a famous essay, Cornel West writes:

> The most significant theme of the new cultural politics of difference is the agency, capacity and ability of human beings who have been culturally degraded, politically oppressed and economically exploited ... This theme neither romanticizes nor idealizes marginalized peoples. Rather it accentuates their humanity. (West 1990, p.34)

This collection of life stories attempts to accentuate the humanity of and the differences between some 14 people who seem to share little except the label of learning disability, and to suggest some ways in which the abuse of that label has led to an erosion of their identities and a restriction on their abilities to exercise choice.

One of the exercises undertaken every year at King Alfred's College, Winchester, by new students on the BA (Hons) Degree in Social and Professional Studies: Learning Disabilities, is to consider pen pictures of two people which are displayed on an overhead projector slide. These two people are usually referred to as Person A and Person B, and the list of traits and characteristics for Person A reads something like this:

Friendly and warm
Good social skills
Is well known in his specialist field
Plays sport at a high level
Unthreatening
Has published articles
Committee member for several community projects

whilst for Person B it reads like this:

Gets irritable
Has unsociable habits
Flits from one job to another before finishing
Has a major heart defect
Loses temper
Often gets people's name wrong
Gets tired after lunch
Overweight

The students are asked to suggest where they might meet a Person A type and a Person B type. Sometimes they guess the outcome quite quickly, but often they create lists of prestigious occupations and places for Person A and an even longer list of institutional settings and syndromes for Person B. The reality is that Person A and Person B are the same, namely Barry Gray, one of the co-editors of this book (although, on better acquaintance, the students dispute the resemblance to Person A). The points that are necessary to make to the students at this stage of their course are that there are different, but equally accurate, ways of describing and writing about people, and that these lead to different views and images.

For people with learning difficulties, and most other devalued and marginalised groups, the written way of describing members of their group tends towards the negative model of the description of Person B. This appears to be particularly true in communication between professionals. The impressions created by such writings can be negative, unhelpful, frightening, and lead to low expectations. Two particular examples demonstrate this point.

The first example involved meeting a young man with learning difficulties in England. The written 'reports' received in advance on this person included these descriptions: 'blind, a messy eater, aggressive, has an IQ in the 30s, very difficult to work with.' Whilst some of this was no doubt true, it did not accurately represent the young man himself. He was indeed blind, and he tried to show people that he did not like being fed certain foods or being fed too quickly. He did not like loud noises or shouting and seemed to get upset when he did not know what was happening. He did like it when people explained what was happening and spoke to him. He seemed to learn things quite quickly and once he had washed, shaved and been dressed in smart and clean clothes, he was a pleasure to work with.

The second example took place in Canada. In response to an expression of interest in the native culture, two sets of source materials were provided. One was a series of case files on native Canadians who were resident in a local institution for people with learning difficulties (called the 'mentally retarded' at this institution). The second was a series of books of fiction, based on native Canadian characters living on one of the reservations, by W. P. Kinsella, perhaps best known as the author of *Shoeless Joe*, which was filmed as *Field of Dreams*.

The first source gave the reader no clues either to the culture of the institution or to the individuals within it. Apart from some differences in spelling and terminology, the material could have come from any British long-stay hospital for people with learning difficulties. The second source was quite different: it gave the impression of an encounter with some real people, and an insight into their way of life. Canadian colleagues have subsequently confirmed that the Kinsella books are indeed a reasonably accurate representation of the native culture of Canada. Clearly the best way to learn about other people is to meet them and get to know them. If this is not possible, then a story that brings the person alive must be preferable to an outline of social skills, IQ scores, personal habits and temperament.

We hope that this collection of stories brings to life for the reader a number of new acquaintances. The stories are written as they were told by the people themselves. Others working in the field have suggested that this exercise has various benefits for the participants involved, (e.g. Gillman, Swain and Heyman 1997; Atkinson 1993). We did not carry out the exercise with any therapeutic goals in mind and do not claim any; we do know, however, that the participants reported having had a good time and fully enjoying themselves.

How the stories were collected

As part of their final year studies on the BA (Hons) Social and Professional Studies: Learning Disabilities, students complete a module entitled 'Life Story – Ethical and Equal Opportunity Issues'. All the students are required to write the life history of someone they know who has learning difficulties, and to set it down, as far as possible, as though it was the person telling their own story. Students then go on to analyse that life history, using frameworks involving an understanding of both ethical and equal opportunity issues.

The students are required to obtain permission from the participants, ensuring that they understand both the purpose of the exercise and to what extent the life history will be read by others. Some students work with people they have known for a reasonable period of time: perhaps someone they have known through employment before coming on the course; perhaps someone with whom they currently work as a part-time employee (it is the norm now for students to have to work whilst they study); or someone a student has met through activities based at the college, and run for local adults with learning difficulties. In other cases, students work with people with whom they have had little previous contact.

Students are then encouraged to explore different methodologies for the collection and presentation of these life stories. Goodley (1996) provides a comprehensive critique of the strengths and weaknesses of life history research. He suggests that one way of working with 'inarticulate people' (as some people with learning difficulties may well be), is to construct a 'lifeplan' (a visual representation of 'good' or 'bad' experiences from birth to the present day) for the person, to be used as a point of reference. We termed this process 'lifemapping', and all students were asked to produce a lifemap of their own, as a starting point, to share with the person with learning difficulties. The lifemaps of the two editors of this collection are shown at the end of this Introduction: there are several similarities between these two lives, despite a difference of four years in age and different places of birth. These similarities include attendance at similar types of school at the same ages, the development of a career, marriage and having a family. In many cases we might expect to find these similarities mirrored in the lifemaps of other white males of the same age: they are the product of the life choices available to this set of people.

There are, moreover, choices open to this generation of males and not to an earlier generation: although both editors are in their 50s, society no longer imposes on them the identity of being old men, as it would have done on men of that age a generation earlier: Western culture now admits of the possibility of role models for men in their 50s who are still active, fit and attractive, whereas a generation earlier there were no equivalents to Mick Jagger or David Bowie.

What is even more striking, however, is that the lifemaps of Barry and Geoff, so similar to each other, are very different from the lifemap of a 50-year-old person with learning disabilities. More challenging still is the question of whether the stories which follow demonstrate that there is a fixed identity imposed by society on all people with learning disabilities, an identity which robs them of life choices, and which, more significantly, has not changed from generation to generation. Barry and Geoff at 50 are allowed to construct identities which are not those of old men: do the younger people whose stories feature in this book have a greater freedom of choice in the construction of their identities than did the older subjects?

Most students used their own lifemaps to stimulate story-telling, and most produced a lifemap on and for the person with learning difficulties: for most of the participants, these have become treasured possessions, and copies are included after most of the life stories. Some lifemaps originally contained photographs, and some were drawn on several large sheets of paper, attached to a wall and then videoed whilst the subjects told their stories using the lifemaps for prompts. Either the subjects or the students supplied the artwork of the lifemaps included in this book.

Atkinson, Jackson and Walmsley (1997) suggest six factors which account for the expansion of interest in the exploration of the life histories of people with learning difficulties. These are:

1. The reappraisal of institutional care following the closure of long-stay hospitals and an emphasis on 'care in the community'.

2. The availability of institutional archives following their closure, which has enabled historians to document accounts of life in these colonies (see Radford and Tipper 1988).

3. The promotion of various types of advocacy for people with learning difficulties, coupled with the increasing perception of the need to use history in order to legitimise claims of marginalisation.

4. Changes in academic history such that the lives and experiences of ordinary and marginalised people have become as much the focus as those of 'great men'.

5. The establishment, within the medical profession, of the field of learning difficulties as a distinct speciality and a legitimate area for scientific study and treatment. This has led to the setting up of academic departments, the

publication of specialist journals, the planning of specific courses of study, and the growth in identifiable careers within human services.

6.   A continuation of the nature versus nurture debate fuelled by recent discussions about the genetic basis of disease and behaviour, which, in turn, have raised the topic of eugenics.

The stories presented in this collection may be seen as part of this expansion of interest. They were collected as part of a specific degree course, attached to an academic department which has learning difficulties as its central focus. Many of the stories refer to life in the long-stay institutions and some highlight errors that we must learn to avoid in the future. Perhaps the most important reason for sharing these stories is that they are accounts of members of society whose biographies are often hidden. They are not meant to represent 'heroes' who have come through all kinds of adversity, nor to portray uncaring communities or an uncaring society. They are stories of people with whom we share our existence, but not, perhaps, our lives. It is for this reason that we made the conscious decision not to preface each story with an explanation of the nature of the learning difficulty of that particular subject: they are, first and foremost, stories of people.

One common factor in this exercise of collecting the life stories was that all the participants were willing and reported that they really enjoyed the time spent with the student sharing information. In exploring the ethical dilemmas in open-ended interviews with people with learning difficulties, Swain, Heyman and Gillman (1998, p.24) suggest that 'the pursuit of ethical ideals is founded on reflections on the decision making processes themselves, the differing vested interests of those involved and the social relations within specific contexts'. Certainly, within this particular project, there was much reflection on the ethical issues involved in students gathering the stories and publishing them. Refreshingly, the students themselves proved to be the fiercest critics of the exercise. They feared that it was going to be a one-way intrusion into the life of another person with no benefit to that person. They could easily identify benefits for themselves, both in gaining credit towards their degrees, and in having the opportunity to spend time with someone they liked, but could see little benefit for the person with learning difficulties. Stalker (1998, p.9) might have agreed with them: 'I was seeking something from them – data – and what exactly they were going to get in return was probably unclear to everyone, including myself'.

Swain *et al.* use the following taxonomy of issues in the ethical analysis of their own research:

1. rationale for undertaking the research

2. respect

3. informed consent

4. privacy

5. confidentiality and anonymity

6. safety

7. exploitation

and it may be useful to employ this same framework in exploring the ethical problems confronted in the course of this project.

Rationale for undertaking the project

It was felt by the course team that this exercise would provide a very powerful way of enabling the students to relate theoretical frameworks of equal opportunities and ethics to the lives of real people. In addition, students would be introduced to some techniques of qualitative data collection and would practise these under supervision. Students would also be able to develop skills in writing, communicating with people with learning difficulties and in negotiation. Moreover, the exercise provided a further way of involving people with learning difficulties in the degree course itself, and this was seen as an effective way of meeting equal opportunities and ethics learning outcomes.

Initially, for the people with learning difficulties who participated in this exercise, justification was provided for them rather than by them. Reading other examples of life stories (e.g. Deacon 1974; Wildey 1985; Humphreys, Evans and Todd 1987; Atkinson and Williams 1990; Atkinson 1993; Ramcharan et al. 1997) we were encouraged to think there would be no reason why this should not be enjoyable and, perhaps, beneficial for the participants. Although we were not attempting to justify the exercise as a therapeutic intervention (cf. White and Epston 1990; Usher 1993), there was a sense in which we all understood that most people enjoy talking about and reflecting on their lives (see Gillman et al. 1997 for a discussion on the benefits of constructing life stories). Students' work on this exercise was regularly supervised and all had developed contingency plans should material be revealed with which they felt unable to cope adequately. Finally, we considered the stories to be important material for a wider audience. Increasingly, the people now entering into human services have no experience of the institutional care regimes of the recent past. The more the challenges of creating a fully inclusive society are recognised and perceived as requiring even more creative solutions, the more crucial it is that we take account of the lessons to be learned from this history.

Respect

Amongst other things, respect is about treating someone in a similar way to any other valued member of society. So, as a beginning, we had to provide opportunities for the students to explore their own values towards people with learning difficulties and other marginalised groups. Much of this work began two years prior to the collection of the life stories and is an on-going process. People with learning difficulties are involved in teaching on the degree programme (see Kirkpatrick and Earwaker 1997) at King Alfred's College, and it is hoped this provides a model that students can explore.

In addition to treating with respect those who told their stories to us, we have also tried to be respectful to the stories themselves. In the Conclusion, we endeavour to offer an analysis of what has been said in the stories, and we have tried to avoid suggesting reasons why we think these things may have been said.

The students collecting the stories quickly learned that respect has to be earned, and that they needed to exercise particular sensitivity when talking to people significantly older than themselves. One way of earning and maintaining respect is to be seen to be listening carefully, and to be acting upon what is heard.

Informed consent

On a simple level, all the participants in the original exercise gave informed consent to be involved in the project and two people signalled their full understanding of the implications of this consent by adding that they did not wish their stories to go to a wider audience than the student and two tutors. We recognise that some of the participants may well have given their consent in order to help the students and that some may not have fully understood the information they were given. The students were conscientious in constantly checking with participants that they agreed to be involved, and in relaying new information as circumstances changed. For example, it became clear at any early stage that the external examiner to the course would need to see a sample of the stories, and this scrutiny had not been agreed by any of the participants at the outset. Where the students were involved with a subject whose communication they did not fully understand, or with a child, then permission was also sought from the appropriate adult.

Privacy

Just how much control the participants had over their involvement once the project was underway is questionable. The pressure for students to complete the module assignment was great and, once the exercise was in progress, they are likely to have employed many subtle conscious and unconscious tactics to ensure it continued to fruition. Certainly no participant withdrew once the project had begun. Two students felt unable to gather a life story from a person with learning difficulties and they carried out their analysis using stories which had already been published.

Problems also arose when subjects disclosed matters which they wished to go no further: on the one hand, students needed to respect such a wish whilst acknowledging that the wish not to disclose constituted, in itself, a part of the data which informed the story; on the other hand, it might be argued that to have had the matter disclosed would have shown more respect to the subject, in the sense that it allowed him/her to voice these concerns.

Confidentiality and anonymity

The process of observing confidentiality is not a simple one: it is not a matter of establishing guidelines at the outset which are then taken as implicit for the rest of time. Confidentiality is a process of continual checking and reassurance.

Anonymity can never be guaranteed absolutely, but the conventional method of changing names of people and places was followed. For some participants this was not what they wanted: they felt ownership of the narrative – it was their story and they wanted it to be told with real names. Even after it was explained that many people named in the story would have no opportunity for reply, some subjects still expressed a wish for there to be no change to their story. However, it seems that either the desire to please the student, or the hope of getting their stories into print, proved too strong, for all those who agreed to publication also eventually agreed to name changes. Part of the encouragement, to gain agreement, was that subjects were urged to choose their own pseudonym and, as a result, several of the participants are eagerly awaiting the publication of their story so they can share it with friends.

We felt that it would be inappropriate to try to edit these very different stories into too rigid a standard format. Where the students have used third-person narrative, we have retained that viewpoint; where the account has been constructed as a first-person narrative, from the viewpoint of the student, we have let that stand.

Safety

The safety issues to be considered include:

- potential dangers of supporting students and people with learning difficulties meeting in unsupervised settings
- handling of sensitive material
- effective 'closing' of the exercise
- maintenance of the relationship between the student and storyteller.

Unsupervised settings

With respect to the first of these subcategories, all the students on this degree programme undergo a police check for previous convictions as a matter of course, and all have experience of working in human services with people with learning difficulties. Although this is not a guarantee of safety for the students or for those with learning difficulties, by the time of this module the students are in their final year of study and have undergone three periods of supervised practice placement, so there will have been several opportunities to ensure that they do not display inappropriate and/or grossly unprofessional behaviours: such action would have led to their being deemed unsuitable for continuing on the course. In addition, most of the partnerships were between people who had known one another for some time, and so there was a reasonable amount of confidence that people were not moving into physically unsafe situations.

Sensitivity

Students were asked to develop a code of practice for dealing with any sensitive issues that might be raised and this code was discussed and refined during tutorial supervision sessions. Many students were anxious about what to do if there were revelations of abuse, and all students were required to demonstrate that they knew who to contact should they feel unable to adequately deal with the situation, or if the volunteer had asked for further professional help. At the very outset, students were encouraged to make the nature of the exercise clear to potential participants, and to indicate clear boundaries for the relationship.

Closure

Work on the third subcategory, effective closing of the exercise, began in the very early stages: for some people, the exercise will not be closed until this book is published; for others, the exercise may have already closed but there continue to be reasons why the student and participant meet. All students were asked to consider what they might present to their volunteer at the end of the exercise. This was seen both as response to the issue of 'What's in it for me?', and also as a concrete way of closing the exercise. The gifts varied and included copies of lifemaps, audiotaped stories, videotapes of stories, photo albums and visits to restaurants.

Maintenance of the relationship between the student and the storyteller

Success in maintaining the relationship between student and volunteer varied greatly: for many participants there was a history to the relationship, in that a future was already anticipated; for a few, the relationship was very temporary. Students on this course are recruited nationally and internationally, and, in some cases, it is unlikely that the participants will have occasion or opportunity to meet again.

Exploitation

Have we exploited the people who agreed to be involved in this exercise by publishing this book? Certainly, we would recognise that it would have been extremely difficult for any of the students to refuse to undertake the assignment attached to this particular module, although, as mentioned earlier, two students did negotiate a shift in the terms of the assessment by working on a story which had already been published. Once underway, moreover, it was perhaps more difficult for the people with learning difficulties to withdraw. We tried to ensure that all those involved were regularly reminded of the voluntary nature of their participation and that they could withdraw at any time. In the end we have used these people's stories for what we suggest and believe are important reasons: the chance to celebrate some of their experiences; the chance for others to learn from these experiences; and the opportunity to gain recognition for these stories as a resource of considerable value and worth. But we still have exploited the participants. Our only excuse and defence is that we did, at least, offer them the choice of being involved in the project or not.

Selection principles

There were over 30 students taking the module which generated the life stories included in this book. Not all the stories collected by students are contained here: we wanted to include stories which were well told, as well as maintaining a balance of gender and a variety of ages and experiences. It is not the case that only the stories collected by the best students found their way into this book: the grading was based upon a range of criteria and not limited to the ability to fashion a good biography. What we have tried to do, however, is to leave the stories as free from editorial intervention as possible. They are arranged according to chronology, with the oldest storyteller coming first: inevitably this means that the stories at the end of the book tend to be shorter because they record briefer lifespans.

Conclusion

One piece of serendipity occurred during the editing of this material, which proved very instructive. We wanted to ensure that no story included the common confusion of 'its' and 'it's' and so we simply entered 'its' in the 'Find' box on our word-processing program and examined each instance for correctness. Because we had not put a space either before or after 'its', we were given, in addition to the words we wanted, all words which included those three letters in that order. What this revealed was the very frequent use of the words 'visit' and 'visits': these terms occur over 30 times in the stories which follow, and we believe that the use of these terms carries very powerful ideological connotations. This can be demonstrated through a quotation from a recent biography of Paul McCartney by Barry Miles, called *Many Years from Now*, in which McCartney has this to say about John Lennon's relationship with his mother:

> I had lost my mum, that's one thing, but for your mum to actually be living somewhere else and for you to be a teenage boy and not living with her is very sad ... John and I would go and visit her and she'd be very nice but when we left there was always a tinge of sadness about

John. On the way back I could always tell that he loved the visit and he loved her but was very sad that he didn't live with her. (Miles 1997, p.48)

It is clear from this brief quotation that visits imply brevity and discontinuity. They are temporary phenomena and are no substitute for a continuing relationship. However, it is also all too evident, in the stories which follow, that there is a substantial group of people whose lives revolve around visits, and visits over which they have no real control.

Figure 1.1 Lifemap – Barry Gray

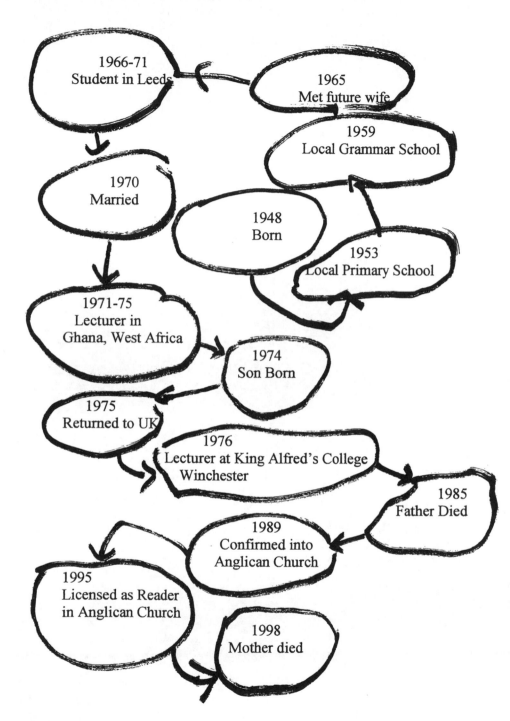

Figure 1.2 Lifemap – Geoff Ridden

2

Mary

This is a story of a woman born in 1927 in Inverness, Scotland. Her mother was Scottish and her father, who was from Somerset, had come to Inverness as an army man. Mary was one of twin girls, born into a large family of eleven children. As a child, she was unaware of the mysteries her own life would bring, the pain, the loneliness, the friendships and the adventures, all the events leading to the comfort and companionship she now enjoys.

Being a twin can bring an intimacy that is special, and the friendship and bonding that Mary and her sister had brought both joy and sadness to them. Naturally, they spent a lot of time together playing and exploring, all the mischief children usually get up to. They both attended the local school where their brothers and sisters also went. Mary says of this time:

> I used to get ill a lot and I couldn't pass my exams, I didn't have much lessons then.

In their teenage years, having moved to the south of England with their family, Mary and her sister played in the streets, went to local dances and enjoyed growing up into young women together. As they entered womanhood, the two sisters attracted the interests of men. This felt perfectly natural as they discovered and explored the joys of adolescence. Dating men brought them fun, laughter and sometimes, inevitably, the tears that relationships can involve. But the sisters, as twins, had a close affinity with and understanding of each other, so they could share their joy and pain. Until one devastating day when, at the age of sixteen, they were separated.

Mary did not understand the reason for this separation and, what made it all the more distressing was that she was sent away, separated from her sister and family, while her sister remained part of the family. Mary realised that her family had not been pleased with her meeting a young man by the fire station some evenings, but could not see why her family had sent her away and not her sister, who had also been meeting a young man.

Mary spent the next two years in a convent, having very little contact with her family. There were other women staying at the convent but she did not know why they were there, any more than she knew why she was there herself. Questions were not encouraged and Mary had to accept this as her new home, although she did not know how long she might be there.

In 1945, when she was eighteen, Mary left the convent and was sent to a large hospital, one of the notorious institutions where people who had been judged a problem lived segregated from the rest of the community. Mary was still only a young woman. She knew no one at the hospital, it was strange and unfamiliar for her, and still she did not understand why she could not be with her family.

She was given a white hospital dress to wear and shown to the ward where ten other women lived. Sometimes it became overcrowded and Mary would sleep on the floor, sometimes with a mattress and sometimes not. She began to make friends, but no one could replace the relationship she had once shared with her sister. Her parents came to visit Mary occasionally but her mother felt uncomfortable and did not like going there. Mary remembers that:

> My mother was scared, some of the women would try to steal her handbag.

As, predictably, the visits became less regular, Mary felt even more cut off from her family. She got on well at the hospital and was allowed to go out sometimes. The staff at the hospital realised that Mary was a very capable woman and would give her jobs to do. In addition, Mary felt fortunate to get some domestic work from people with houses near the hospital, and she would spend a lot of her time at these houses, so that she would not have to spend so much time in the ward. Sometimes she was able to stay overnight.

Mary remembers that people living in the hospital sometimes got punished if they were 'bad'. She herself did not get into trouble very often:

> I had seen the reports from the doctors, me not being naughty like the others had done,

she recalls.

Mary does, however, remember one night when a woman from her ward ran away from the hospital and made her way to the bus station. But, as she was crossing the road, the woman was hit by a bus and was killed. Mary remembers that the night staff, who should have locked the doors, tried to blame the accident on Mary and two other women on the ward. As punishment, these three women were not allowed to go out for the following week.

Mary and a friend of hers from hospital longed for the freedom that they remembered, the freedom to be able to do as they wished and to not have to stay at the hospital. Mary hated to stay indoors all the time – it would give her a headache – and so, one sunny spring day, the two friends did not go back to the hospital but decided instead to run away. They were missing in Portsmouth for a few days, but some people who Mary worked for came to pick them up and took them back. Mary recounts this incident in a healthy, rebellious and joyous way.

She has some bad memories of the 13 years that she spent at hospital, including some of experiences which were very unpleasant and scarred her permanently. Mary realises that there were other patients at the hospital treated far worse than she was, because they 'misbehaved'. Of these patients, Mary says:

> Some people had to take drugs to make them dopey and some people were locked away at times when they were very bad.

Eventually, Mary left hospital, and she gives this explanation of the reason she had to move out:

> There were too much people there and they started closing the hospital down so I had to leave.

She remembers very clearly the life of disruption which followed:

> I have lived in lots of homes, I can't remember all of them.

One of the houses she lived in was a group home, but she got fed up there. Mary needed more independence and would get fed up and frustrated with staff watching over her when she felt quite capable of doing things on her own. She moved into a flat, and that was where she met Albert: they had known each other for about a year when they decided to get married.

Mary wished to see more of her brothers and sisters, and to rebuild the bond between them. Some of the family had moved to America, but Mary did not let distance deter her from seeing her relatives. When Mary and Albert were married in 1991, she wore a beautiful outfit she had acquired on one of her trips to America:

> I had a pink hat, a pink dress and a pink garter. I got embarrassed when they wanted to see my garter at the wedding,

Mary laughed. She had longed to be like her sisters who were married and had children.

> I was the last one to get married, I always wanted to get married.

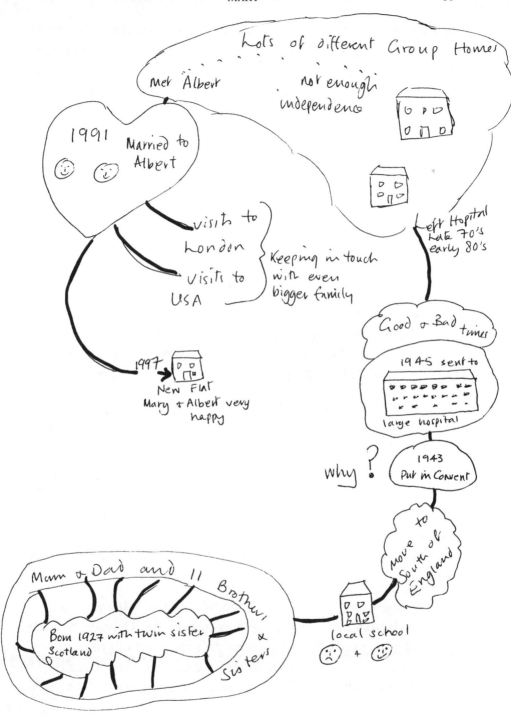

Figure 2.1 Lifemap – Mary

Mary has had many adventures and reunions visiting her family in America and spending time with her twin sister in London. Her family has grown enormously from eleven brothers and sisters, and she now has many nieces and nephews. Mary has never had children of her own but can now enjoy being a much-loved aunt.

Mary and Albert have recently moved into a flat where there is a warden and where they are visited most days by a support worker. Mary was glad to leave the previous flat and to have the security of their present home because at the last place she used to get scared:

> The children used to upset me, the neighbours, the girls they were pests, they were always nosing in. They stole some of my money. The police didn't believe what I said. They kept asking me questions. They only want me to go to a court place to answer questions. But I didn't want to go, I don't like courts.

The new flat is in a peaceful area, and has an intercom door-answering system which Mary operates with confidence and which gives her the peace of mind that no one can come up uninvited. Mary and Albert are very happy there together. Like any couple, they have the occasional disagreement, but they enjoy an active social life, visiting friends, going out for lunch and organising their home.

At the age of 70, Mary still does not understand why she was sent away when none of her sisters were:

> They never been in the homes, that's what I can't understand. My sisters were as bad as me. They used to play up like hell but Dad wouldn't say anything to them, only to me. I was shut in and I can't get over it really. Because why should I suffer and not the others?

3

Margaret

I have known Margaret for about six years now and over this time I have always been aware of, and very impressed with, her memory, both for historical events, and for the way she could tell stories about her childhood. Her life gave me a real insight into a world I could never enter, the world of the patient in a long-term hospital for the 'mentally handicapped'.

I was very sad to find, therefore, when I actually came to tape her story, that she showed signs of having lost or forgotten many of those memories. For this reason, whilst her story still gives insights into her life, it no longer paints the rich picture that I had glimpsed in earlier conversations. Whether this is through deliberate choice or not, I am not sure. It may result from the circumstances of her talking about herself: when she is specifically asked about events, it may be that she consciously decides then to focus on the good times of her life. But one of the reasons I suspect that this is not simply a deliberate choice is that she is beginning to get dates wrong. For example, during the taping of the interviews, she mixed up the dates of the Second World War and of decimalisation. There was a time not so long ago when any date in history or the birthday of anyone she knew came readily to her lips.

During the past ten years she has, at various times, received counselling from a psychologist and, as a result of these sessions, certain kinds of questioning can make her very agitated and upset. It seems that the attempt to pursue her past, and thus enable her 'to come to terms' with her early life, has not been terribly useful or helpful to her.

Margaret's mother was 18 years old when she was born. Her mother has Down's syndrome, had been sexually abused by her father and Margaret had been the result. It has never been clearly established exactly what Margaret knows and understands about her parentage: her mother is always referred to as 'mum', her grandmother as 'gran' but her father is referred to both as 'dad' and as 'granddad'. There is no pattern to this changing reference to suggest either that she saw him as two people changing with the situation (e.g. 'dad' in good times and 'granddad' in bad, or *vice versa*), or as one person who just happened to have two names. Throughout this life story, he will be referred to as 'grand/father' when he is mentioned in my narrative, and, in direct quotations from Margaret, by whichever title she gives him at that particular time.

Margaret's story seemed to get worse each time I reflected upon it. Very little of it is documented in a readily accessible and verifiable form, and so, although most of the story derives from taped interview, a colleague, who has known Margaret's family for a long time and is living in the same village as her family, provided confirmation that most of what Margaret said of her life is true.

Margaret's story begins with this extraordinary claim:

> My first memory is coming out into the open. On my mummy's lap, when I was born and all the family round me … yes … it was a nice time but there were no photographer there to take a photo … no … I can remember the midwife taking me to the kiss-of-life table. Giving me the kiss-of-life, and then she took me back to mum who gave me my first milk feed. And then I was originated to Berkshire straight after that. Yes … mum took me to Berkshire. In one of those old fashioned taxi cabs that they used, after that.

Margaret was born in September 1934. She has no brothers or sisters but has eight cousins with whom she played as a small child:

> I remember Christmases from when I was little, and Easters and Whitsuntide. I can remember the first Christmas present I had: a beautiful big brown rabbit with a pink bow and big brown eyes, and visits to the pantomime with Gran and Gran's friend. We saw *Cinderella, Babes in the Wood* and *Dick Whittington.*

She was a pupil at the local primary school, and remembers this as a happy time. But, although Margaret enjoyed her school life, her mother

> had to leave me at home when I was six with dad and gran – she had to leave me when I was six to go to these places to earn a living and to be looked after as well – my mum.

She remembers her teachers by name and remembers being taught to knit by an older pupil.

She then went on to the local secondary modern school which she again enjoyed and

> no way did I ever need the cane! I was good all the time there. I got a star for good progress in the English lesson.

At about this time Margaret was also doing jobs for a local lady – housework and cleaning – which she didn't enjoy and didn't get paid for but

> I did it out of the kindness of my heart!

At around the age of 13, Margaret moved to a convent in London:

> I don't know why I went to the convent – to be looked after I think – according to my mum and dad and gran … to be looked after.

There is some suggestion that her grand/father started to inter-
fere with her at around this time, but Margaret never refers to this.
Instead, she recalls that she

> stayed in the place and they took me for walks on the
> Sunday afternoon in my summer dresses and that, I went
> to their chapel as well, I stayed there for holidays and three
> Christmases.

The happy times were:

> going to church – to help them with their singing – a
> Catholic church. I had a nice bed to sleep in, in a
> dormitory with 14 girls. They were nice girls, they were
> fond of me. The girls in the other cottages weren't as nice
> in OL's cottage and SJ's cottage. They weren't so nice as
> the ones in SHJ's cottage – they were very nice to me but
> the others weren't. I liked the statue of Our Lady in the
> leisure court there. Yes, near the field where the swings
> were. But towards the end of my time there the girls in the
> convent made my nerves bad … yes … um, after three
> years there.

She learned English, arithmetic, history, geography, cookery and
sewing and, at the age of 16, she left and went on to another convent near St Albans. She is unsure why she left but seemed to
think, as we talked about it, that everybody left that school at 16
years of age. She describes the new convent as a:

> training centre convent, where they taught me how to
> work. We learnt housework – yes we had old fashioned
> scrubbing brushes there that they use to do … and
> polishing and that and cleaning the bedrooms, yes they
> showed me how to clean the rooms and that there. They
> were kind to me, they weren't cruel at all.

I asked her if she felt that she needed to go to the hospital,
whether she thought she could have coped on her own:

No, I would have coped all right if the girls had left me alone, I would have coped all right.

Margaret seems to have kept in regular contact with her immediate family:

Yes, I had contact with them and I used to write to them and dad wrote me a postcard to say gran had passed peacefully away. I was at the convent then in St Albans, she died on 26 November 1951. She sang 'Good King Wenceslas' to me one Christmas when I lived at home with her and dad, she sang to me in a very nice way – that's my happiest thought about my gran that I can remember.

What about mum?

Mum didn't have much chance because my father knocked her about. He started the same thing on me and my mum took it further – she did something about it – she called the police, they took my dad away – he'd begun to be cruel to me. He started the same thing on gran and then my mum hit the nail on the head when he started on me – mum did something about it – she got the police to him. Yes … um, they took him away – my mum gave evidence about it to the police. My mum told the police … um, but the kind thing my dad did was when he rubbed my hands in 1939 just before the Second World War started when I was sat in front of the fireplace, an old-fashioned fireplace in the kitchen.

It is believed that at this time grand/father did go away, but it is not known where to or for what reason, or how long.

Although Margaret enjoyed her time at St Albans it was alleged that she stole sixpence and, as a result, she was sent to hospital. When she talks about the move she says that she left after just over three years 'cos the girls kept aggravating me, towards the end of my time there so they placed me in hospital to be looked after.

When asked specifically about the incident with the sixpence she gets very agitated and denies stealing anything. Her own account of the hospital is that she

> did 20 years there. I went because my nerves were bad … yes … um, but after 24 years they got better: they made a vast improvement. They had wards there – wards – I first went there to 11b and the doctor looked at me and said I was in good condition. They put me on sedatives to calm my nerves, they got better and I started to make my way out a bit – go to the hairdresser's, go to work then to the hostel where I waited for four years – I waited there for four years from 1974 to '78, yes, then I came nearer to mum after that.
>
> At the hospital I did sewing, occupation work, writing to mum … and … um laying the tables in the evening and in the morning for breakfast – laying the tables … um, cleaning the toilets – that was the last job I had – cleaning the toilets … and, then in the dormitory and after that they asked me this question – would I like to live nearer to mum and they made the possibilities to do that.

In 1980 Margaret had a short trial in a hostel in North Oxfordshire, but she did not like it there and subsequently moved to her present accommodation.

During her early years at her current home, the manager sexually abused quite a number of the residents, including Margaret. Although several of the residents gave evidence in court against the manager, he was never charged with sexual abuse; he did get a three-month sentence for hitting and kicking a male resident. At the time Margaret denied being involved in the abuse, but, after the trial was over, she became very anxious about it, so the police returned and allowed her to make a full statement. This seems to have helped her put the issue behind her, but she does mention it from time to time, as this short conversation indicates.

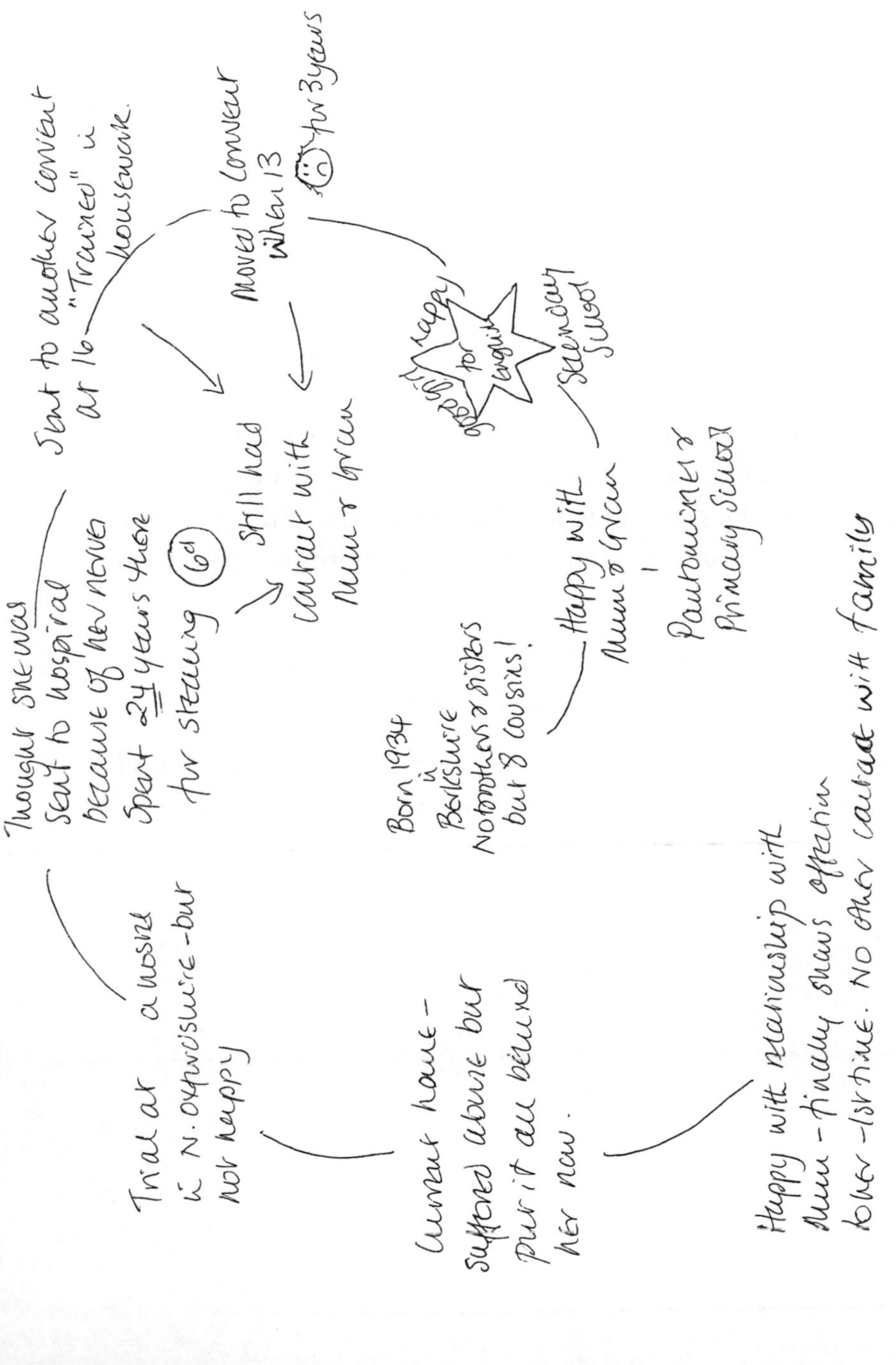

Figure 3.1 Lifemap—Margaret

Thought she was sent to hospital because of her move. Spent 24 years there for stealing 6d

Sent to another convent at 16 "Trained" in housework.

Moved to convent when 13

:) for 3 years

Still had contact with Mum & Gran

Trial at a hostel in Oxfordshire - but not happy

Current home - suffered abuse but put it all behind her now.

Born 1934 in Berkshire No brothers or sisters but 8 cousins!

Happy with Mum & Gran

grateful for tongue - happy

Saturday school

Pangbourne Primary School

Happy with relationship with Mum - finally shows affection towards - 1st time. No other contact with family

We were walking through town one day when we saw a cat in the window of a house, Margaret said:

> I wish we'd had a cat at [home], we had a dog when ————— was manager, I didn't like it when he did things to me when he used to come into my room at night, I didn't like what he did to me. Why did he always save me for Christmas?

Margaret recently came back from the bus stop, having seen her mum off. She was really pleased and excited as mum had 'put her arm round her at the bus station'. In all our interviews, this was the first time Margaret had ever referred to her mum showing her any physical affection.

Margaret visits the graves of her gran and grand/father once a year around November time, accompanied by a staff member. While she is there, she has a long chat with them, telling them all her news, calling her grand/father both dad and granddad, sometimes in the same sentence. She knows she still has relatives living in a nearby town, but they will have nothing to do with her:

> I know I've got aunties living in ————— but I haven't seen them for many years – I don't know why really!

It seems that they have threatened her mum that, if she ever tells Margaret where they live, they will never come to see her again.

4

Peter

The following chapter describes the life history of Peter as he told it to me during two interviews held at the house in Hampshire where he lives.

I was put in contact with Peter through a colleague of mine who knew him well and thought he would welcome this opportunity to share his life story. I then telephoned him, explaining who I was and what this task would entail. Peter agreed and we then arranged a time to 'meet and greet' one another. Before making this arrangement, I had already checked with the manager of his house whether, in order to avoid any potential legal problems, there was anyone else I should contact. I also emphasised the private and confidential nature of the process: anything Peter told me would be treated with the strictest respect.

The report is written from Peter's perspective, as a reflection of how he has seen his life. As the interviewer, I made every effort to clarify his story with him by listening carefully and asking him questions, not only to help my understanding, but also as a method of cross-checking with him that what I was writing down was an accurate account, recorded as he would wish it to be.

There are certain areas of the report that remain unclear, mainly because his memory is a little cloudy, and because it is a difficult job for anyone to recall one's life history. However, what follows is as accurate an account as was possible under the circumstances. The validity of some of the data may be questionable, but I did not wish to challenge Peter's ability to tell me a story that first, is very precious, and second, that I felt very honoured and privileged to hear. As is the norm with all good practice on the issue of confidentiality, all names have been changed.

The first and only child of Robert and Lilly, Peter was born into the world in January 1941 at a hospital in Surrey. Sometime after his birth (Peter could not recall precisely the actual time), his family moved to Hampshire, and, following this move, there seems to have been a break-up of the family unit. This is an assumption on my part based on Peter's clear remembrance that:

> I lived with my mum at number seven and my dad lived at number ten.

Peter offered no further explanation or elaboration beyond this statement, but did not seem at all perturbed by what it implied. I did not pursue the issue for fear of exposing him to something he might wish to forget.

Peter has no recollection of attending a nursery school prior to starting at his local infant school when he was five years old. But starting school was an experience he remembers as totally negative. He recalls having only one friend at this time, whose name was Andrew. When I asked why he felt he had no other friends, he replied that:

> no one will play football with you when you only have one good arm.

Peter attended this school for only one year before transferring to another school which he attended for the next ten years; he remembers this as a happy time. He had four friends who were in his class, with whom he used to play and eat his dinner, and Peter remembers that he used to read and write outside in the playground whilst the other children were inside. He also recalls that he used to go out shopping for the teachers. He would buy milk and bread and felt very honoured that he was the only one felt to be responsible enough to do this.

However, when Peter was ten years old, he began to suffer from epilepsy and, for a while, he was admitted to hospital. After this he was a little less able, and had to be careful what he did. He remembers spending a lot of time sewing in the classroom by himself whilst all the other children did other activities. Peter's mother taught him to sew, and it is an activity he still greatly enjoys.

But he also recalls one teacher who picked on him whenever she found him in the classroom sewing. Peter does not remember the reasoning behind this, but he speaks of her with evident dislike.

Peter left school at 17 years of age and I have made the assumption that he may have had to repeat one or two years. When he left he did not go on to any further training or education, such as an adult training centre, but continued instead to live at home with his mother. He describes this as being another very happy time in his life.

Lilly did not work, but Peter would go shopping for her, buying the Sunday and weekday papers and anything else that they needed. Peter and his mother were clearly very close, and the two of them would often go for days out, especially to local seaside resorts. Peter enjoyed these trips, paddling on the beach and watching the television in cafes, while they were having their tea.

Peter also remembers that, during this period when he was living at home, he would travel to a nearby town on Tuesdays and Thursdays to visit the theatre and to see shows with both his mother and his father. Sometimes they were musical shows, and sometimes drama, but he liked them all.

It is not clear just how long Peter lived at home with his mother, but the significant stage in his story centres around the death of his mother, which he obviously recalls with great sadness. He remembers the build-up to his mother's death, as her health declined over a period of some time. He found this period very traumatic, and he was so frightened about what would happen that the stress and worry caused his fits to return. Peter was therefore admitted to hospital where his fits could be monitored. He recalls being there for a while, but he did not mind it too much as he had his own room with a television.

On his return from hospital, Peter went back to live in Hampshire in his mother's house. He stayed there by himself, but he remembers having people coming in on a daily basis to help with the cooking and the cleaning. At this stage he was still able to go into town independently, but, after having a 'rather bad turn', he was readmitted to hospital and the question of his continuing to live independently was put under review.

Subsequent to this review, Peter went to live in a large town with his aunt. Again he recalls this with much happiness, remembering specifically the time he and his aunt visited the Picture Palace. However, this was only a temporary arrangement until a placement could be found in which Peter would live permanently.

That placement was eventually found in central Hampshire: he was to live in a bungalow with four other residents. Once more the actual time span of the period preceding this move is not clear, but Peter remained at the bungalow for some fifteen years, making good friends with a number of his house-mates. He recalls one friend in particular, David, whom Peter describes as his best friend: the two of them often had days out together, usually Wednesdays or Thursdays. He remembered that one day they went on a visit where they saw lots of animals.

Although Peter made some good friends at the bungalow, he says that he did not really enjoy living there. However, since it was the only place that was vacant, he had no choice. Peter says that he did not get on with Phil, one of his house-mates, who caused a great deal of trouble, so much so, indeed, that Peter asked if he could be moved to another house. But, before this request was made, an incident occurred that subsequently altered the path of Peter's life.

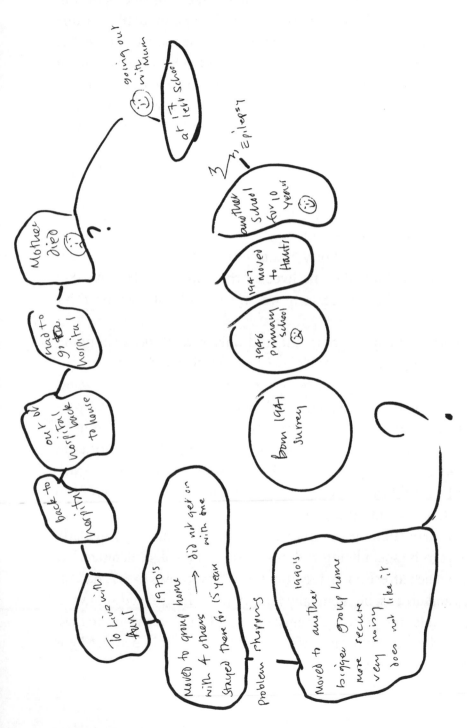

Figure 4.1 Lifemap – Peter

All the time Peter was living at the bungalow he was still actively independent, and often went out unassisted. On one occasion, Peter recalls that he was out shopping when he suddenly became rather agitated. The sequence of events that took place next is slightly unclear but the outcome was that Peter had accidentally knocked someone over, causing them to become unconscious. He was quite upset about the whole situation and unsure of what was happening at the time. And in fact, still recalls the situation with much distress.

What followed as a result of this incident is that Peter lost his independence; he has had to move to a house in a different town, which is not only bigger, and thus has a greater number of residents, but also offers less independence. Peter is not happy living here: he finds it very noisy and misses his friends and the independence he had when he lived in the bungalow. He says that even though he wanted to move, this would not have been his choice.

Peter still enjoys going out, and once a week goes shopping with his support worker. He says he looks forward to these visits but misses not being able to pop to a shop as and when he wants something. He does not enjoy relying on others as this usually results in him missing out. Peter says he is not happy about the decision to take away his independence and wants the authorities to rectify this. He says every time he asks someone what is happening he is told that he will be assessed again soon. This has been going on for almost a year.

On reflection, Peter remembers his life as happy, particularly the years he spent living with his mother, and still remembers her with much affection. Aside from this, Peter knows he has had his ups and downs, but generally feels that life has treated him well, even under the present circumstances. In fact, Peter seems to have learned to accept his loss of independence, mainly because he is powerless to do anything else.

5

Len

Len was born in 1946 in Hampshire. His early life seems to have been quite conventional: he went to the local secondary school, where he remembers doing woodwork and carpentry, and he left as soon as he could just after he was 15. He then enrolled on a day-release course at technical college which he completed in 1966, with a City and Guilds qualification in carpentry.

He started work as a carpenter, but found the job arduous and started suffering from 'bad nerves'. He felt unwell, and started having 'the shakes': he began hearing voices and having strange thoughts which he found very disturbing. Although he completed his apprenticeship and moved firms, he had real difficulty in continuing at work because of the voices.

According to Len's own account, 'They say I am a psychopath'. He has, in fact, been diagnosed as schizophrenic. When the illness became progressively worse, Len consulted a doctor, who gave him some tablets. Len does not believe that this medication made much difference and, in the end, the doctor wrote to a nearby psychiatric hospital. When the consultant psychiatrist came to see him at home and Len told him how he felt, the psychiatrist admitted him to the hospital. This was when Len was about 22 years old.

When Len was first admitted to the hospital, because he was hearing 'nasty voices', he was told that he would be there for only a short time. But, after a few weeks, they moved him from the short-stay ward to the main hospital, where the long-stay wards are situated. The doctor in charge simply told Len that he was not a short-stay patient, and moved him: Len had no choice in the matter.

He lived in several different wards, starting with the admission ward. When he got fed up with one ward, he was allowed to move on to another. However, he was on one particular long-stay ward for seventeen years, until, when he was forty, that ward was closed because its hygiene standards were poor. He spent one further year in hospital, before some social workers came to tell the patients that they were moving to a new group home.

When he was first admitted to hospital, Len remembers feeling 'yucky'. He did not find all of the people there friendly, and, although he believes that he really went into hospital for a rest, he received electric treatment, ECT, to help his depression. Len did not object to this treatment, which involved his being put to sleep: his permission was asked, and he was given treatment sessions of four to six hours, twice a week for three weeks.

Len recalls that, after the treatment, he would wake up with a headache: he used to come round and have four valium. The staff would go around the hospital picking up the patients and taking them up to the top of the building where they received their ECT. There was a waiting room, then when it was all over they would take them back. There were wards all around the grounds.

Len feels that the time he spent in hospital on the long-stay ward went quite quickly. During the day he used to visit the occupational therapist and go to the patients' bank where he could get his money, and every day he went to the shop to get his tobacco. He earned £2.00 a day in the industrial unit where he used to work. They never gave him a lot of work: he could do the job, but it took him a long time. He used to make shrub-tubs to put flowers in: they were made out of cedar wood and then varnished and sold. He used to go to the social centre for a cup of tea, a game of cards, and to put some records on, but mostly for company, as he did not have many friends.

A lot of the patients had trouble with their eyesight because of their medication, but Len had full eyesight all the time he was in hospital. Another side-effect of the medication seemed to be that patients did not get on very well together. However, the other patients eventually got used to Len, although some of them were rather aggressive. They were given other tablets to stop the aggression, to keep them tranquil, and Len thought those tablets worked.

Len suffered from depression during his years in hospital, but he carried on:

> I don't know how I survived it in there.

He says it was his mum and brother that got him through, even though they did not visit him very often. His father died of a stroke, but Len did not go to the funeral: he was told that he would not like it.

His mother was in the same hospital as Len for ten years, and he used to visit her on her ward. She visited him recently with his brother, Robin: she is now eighty-one years old and cannot get about very well:

> It was good to see her, she's a lot better than she was, but she's getting on a bit, and can't do things like she used to.

Len had known three years in advance that the hospital was going to be closed. He felt sad, because he liked it there and he did not want to move to the group home. When the hospital was closing, he moved from the ward where he had spent seventeen years to a different ward, because they started demolishing the other buildings while there were patients still living there.

Len has mixed feelings about life in 'the outside world': he says that everything rushes around and he feels he is just sitting down with life passing him by. On the other hand, Len says he likes it that way!

At the time he was due to move from the hospital, some of the staff from the home used to come up and see him; they bought a paint card so he could choose what colour he wanted his room painted, and also some samples of carpet. It was good to be able to choose a colour, but Len was not allowed to choose the people whom he would live with. There were seven people who were placed together in the group home, some of whom had known each other for years as they had been on the same ward. Others, however, had been on different wards and came with a different range of experiences.

On the day of the move itself, the patients travelled in a coach, each with their belongings in a plastic bag with their name on it, a piece of string and a tag. Len remembers that he was very constipated that day: the doctor changed his medication, but Len did not know what the tablets were, because it had not been explained to him. Len has suffered for forty years with constipation, and he feels that, if he did not like something, he ought to be allowed to say so.

Len both likes and trusts his doctors. He still takes medication, although the dosage has changed: he used to take four doses a day of one drug, but now takes only one dose a day in the morning. He feels it has made his eyesight better:

> You need your eyesight … A lot of the doctors always ask how your bowels are, it's something to do with your bladder and it affects your mind and it's a bit of a sod sometimes.

Len has had his medication changed recently, and that makes him worried and depressed. When last we spoke, he said he felt happy at the moment, although he had not been well on the previous morning which was his birthday. He felt all right in the afternoon:

> The tablets they put in your food, but some food doesn't agree with you and the mixture of the food and

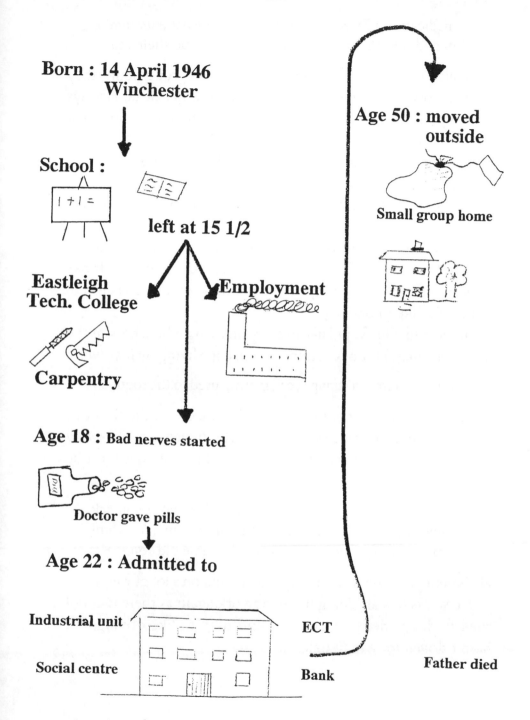

Figure 5.1 Lifemap – Len

> medication affects your head. There were patients coming
> in and out, the same ones every week to be sheltered.

He feels the other men do not like him in the group home: they
are their own worst enemies, wanting each other dead. He says
they have now got used to each other but there is no love lost
between them.

Now he is out of hospital, Len enjoys life and says he has not
changed much in the recent past. He goes into town by taxi to get
his social security. He likes the Spice Girls and the television. He
also likes the Beatles and the Rolling Stones.

He used to walk down to a pub near the hospital sometimes,
although not very often. He does not do that now, and drinks
only shandy. He does not go to the pub now that he has moved,
but might like to one day.

In the future he would like to carry on living where he is, as the
people are nice. He doesn't think he can cope living on his own:

> It's been rather a strange year, getting used to the routine.

He likes routine and tries to get through from one day to the next.
He just about manages to survive. Everybody gets a bit browned
off sometimes and when this happens to Len, he goes for a lie
down.

> The thought pattern inside your head that makes you tick,
> think, right in the middle of the mind, you can't think
> straight, you cannot put up with the same old routine.

He is better than he was, although he has put on a lot of weight.

He wants to start doing his woodwork again as there is a tool
shed in the garden. He likes cars and used to like driving, but
hasn't driven for a long time.

6

Lisa

Lisa was born in June 1950. She spent the first two years of her life with her mother and father in a small village outside one of the major ports in the south of England. Lisa is the younger of two girls, having a sister five years her senior.

Lisa is very proud of the fact that her family has rich historical naval links, one of her ancestors being a famous explorer, and her father a well-known naval commander of his time. Lisa suggests that her earliest years where probably spent around the ports with her father, mother and sister. Photographs from the period show the family having picnics on the coast together when her father was home from sea. Lisa doesn't really remember much about her father's work, although she does think that her mother might have mentioned how often he was away at sea, 'and the war and things'.

In 1953 the family uprooted and moved to one of the largest of the Channel Islands. Lisa doesn't remember why they moved except that they 'took all their things' and started afresh: she thinks, however, that it may have been due to her father's employment circumstances. The family bought a small granite cottage in one of the smaller coastal parishes of the island, about five minutes from the sea. Lisa's most prominent recollections of the house were that it was cold and dark, especially in the winter.

Lisa's earliest childhood memories go back to her days at the parish's nursery and play school. She remembers that she did not stay there very long, mainly because, as she recalls, the other children used to pick on her because she 'was different', and was 'smaller than they were'. She becomes quite emotional as she tells how she often got 'left out' when the other children were playing games, but that she did not know why. Although she recalls being unhappy at the nursery school she also remembers being upset when her parents stopped her from going, because she said it was 'the only chance' that she had to 'go out'.

For several years after leaving the nursery school, Lisa did not attend any educational establishment, because, as she puts it, there was 'nowhere' for her 'to go' because she 'couldn't read and write things as fast as the rest of them'. Lisa recalls spending most of the time at home with her mother, who taught her to look after the house and to do all the household chores, including cleaning, cooking, sewing and embroidery.

In 1959 Lisa's mother died, a subject which was not discussed in any depth for a variety of reasons, including the fact that, in the past, this is an issue which has caused Lisa a great deal of distress. Her life became very different, in that, effectively, Lisa became 'mum', probably because her sister was at school all the time. She started doing all the things around the house, and had to 'look after' her dad. Lisa's sister suggests that Lisa became very independent at this point, doing all the shopping and enjoying walking around the parish talking to people. Lisa recalls getting to know lots of people, and implies that she enjoyed the responsibility and attention that she got. Although her father would not allow her to go into the town centre because she was too young, she still liked getting out and about in the parish and socialising. She does not, however, recall having any friends of her age.

When Lisa was about ten years old, a new school was set up on the island designed to accommodate the educational needs of 'special children' (this phrase was incorporated into the name of the school), and Lisa became one of its first ever pupils. The school was, at the time, as Lisa's sister recalls, 'desperately needed' since there were so many special children 'hidden away in families, unable to be educated in run of the mill schools'. The school was heralded an overwhelming success, the individual who set it up receiving an MBE for her charitable work.

Lisa recalls her time at the school cheerfully, mentioning that the teachers would 'go slowly there'. She learned to read and to write things like her name and her address. She also remarks that many of her closest friends that she still spends time with came from that school, one of whom she is presently living with. Lisa comments that, although she did not mind it too much at home with her dad, she much preferred to go to school, and to get away from the house and into the company of her friends.

Like her peers, Lisa left the 'special school' at sixteen and started straightaway, full time, at the island's adult day service for people with learning disabilities. Her job was to print invitations and 'things like that'. However, after a while these activities dwindled, and most of her day was spent doing 'boring work', like 'taking stamps off envelopes'.

Lisa found the day centre noisy, and feels now that she was there for a very long time doing something that she did not want to do. She realises, however, that she could not get the job that she wanted, so she had no choice but to stay there. The only positive thing about her time at the centre she says was that she got 'a bit' of money and saw her friends. Lisa's ideal job at this point she says would have been to work in a shop like the 'Body Shop', where they did 'make up and hair things'.

Lisa recalls that, when her sister got married and moved to the mainland for five years, she had to do a lot more to look after her dad, because he was not well. She recalls that she 'had to do everything then', for example the 'cleaning and washing'. In 1991, however, he became far too ill for her to cope, and had to be taken into an elderly person's home. Lisa says that she did not mind the fact that he had to go away to live, but she was upset and annoyed that she had to go and live with her sister, who had moved back to the island. Lisa had wanted to live on her own in her house.

While she was living with her sister, Lisa was offered the opportunity to spend short periods of time at a residential home for adults with learning disabilities. She says that she enjoyed her time there, because it gave her the chance to do the things that she wanted to do, such as being able her to meet her friends, go into towns, go to the pub and go to the country and western club. Lisa's aim in life, her sister noted, was to move into the residential home on a permanent basis. When Lisa's father died, at the end of 1991, this became possible, and she was offered the opportunity to move in to the main residential unit full time. However, Lisa recalls not being entirely happy once she was there all the time, finding the place rather noisy, and there being too many people.

Within a couple of months therefore, she was offered the alternative of moving into one of the flats managed by the same residential organisation. Lisa moved into the flat in March of 1992, sharing it with two of her best friends, all of whom had chosen to be together. The flat, although integrated upon the site of the larger residential unit, was designed to offer its residents greater independence, whilst providing the staff support to prepare the individuals with the practical skills and social encouragement to live in more integrated settings.

Lisa recalls the flat being a lot quieter and 'free'. She says that she liked doing things herself, and going into town with her friends when she wanted to. In March of 1995 Lisa made the decision to move into a group house where she was given the opportunity to manage her own home and its finances, along with three other chosen house-mates. She recalls that one of the things she really enjoyed about the move was going out shopping with lots of money to chose all the furniture, and deciding how she would decorate her room. Lisa's sister recalls a distinct change in Lisa's personality at this point: she refers to a sudden growth in

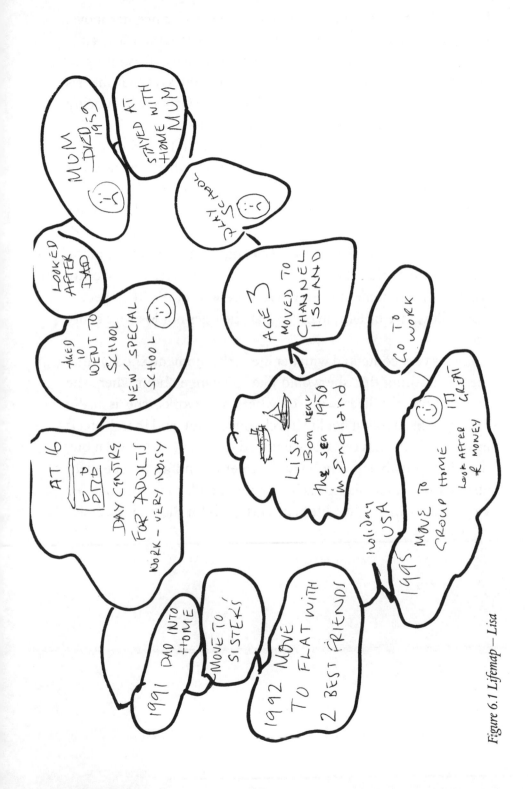

Figure 6.1 Lifemap – Lisa

her confidence and self-esteem, and notes that, since her move, she appears happier and laughs more. Lisa says that she 'loves it'!

Lisa's daily activities, however, have been very frustrating to her, and have made her very angry at times. She says that she has had to wait a long time to get the job that she wants, whilst being 'bored' with 'nothing to do' at the day centre.

She has been working for a cooperative style sheltered employment organisation for the last two years, where she uses her skills as an embroiderer to make things which are then sold in various places across the island. She says that she has always wanted to work somewhere like this, and at last enjoys her work thoroughly. Lisa has just started a cleaning job at an office in the town centre, which she does one day a week. Her total weekly wage at the moment, however, has to be within the 'therapeutic' wage allowance of £44, in order that she does not lose her benefits.

Lisa is very contented with her life at the moment: she says that there is nothing that she would like to change about where she lives, whom she lives with, or where she works, she is really 'happy'. She says that her life has changed 'a lot' and that she feels more 'free'. She has especially enjoyed the chance to travel more, the highlights being a holiday to America and an independent visit to the UK mainland. Each year she spends time with her key worker formulating her 'life plan' and goals for the year to come.

7

Madge

Madge was born in 1950 as the only daughter in a family living in a small village in Hampshire. Her father was a taxi driver and also owned a garage business, with which her mother helped. They have two sons; John was born in 1946 and Peter in 1948.

When Madge was born, her mother was told by a doctor that the baby had slight brain damage which caused her left arm not to move. Apart from that she seemed to be a very healthy baby. However, when she started walking, her parents noticed that she often fell down and was unsteady on her legs. This was caused by uneven leg length and small epileptic fits. At the time, however, little was known about epilepsy and it went undiagnosed until she was four years old. Eventually, her doctor ascertained that Madge was epileptic and told her parents; in addition, her left leg was growing more slowly than her right, so she had to wear special shoes.

Despite these impairments, Madge made some friends who lived near her house and played with them, and she still occasionally sees a couple of them. At the age of five, she started at the local mainstream primary school. Her two brothers had already started school and she had heard a lot about it, so she was really looking forward to going. Although the school was just down the road from her house, she was not allowed to go by herself. Her mother normally took her to school and collected her. Sometimes her friends came around to go to school together. Madge felt that she wanted to go to school by herself like her brothers, but her mother was worried and did not allow that – understandably, given her concern about Madge's epilepsy.

However, Madge probably missed some opportunities to play with her friends as most children do on the way back from school. When Madge was seven years old, she had an operation on her left leg which involved her spending six months, including Christmas, in hospital. Her mother came to visit her every day, and she had a lot of other visitors. She commented that she really missed home at first, but eventually got used to being at hospital.

After this operation, Madge's legs started to grow evenly and, upon leaving the hospital, Madge went back to her school, where she stayed until 1960. However, even during this time, she was often sent back home because of her epileptic fits. Madge told me that she wanted to stay at school because none of her fits were serious, and that if she had stayed, she could have learned more. Her mother comments: 'It was a real shame that Madge missed out on a lot of her education.' It is arguable that her school could have done more to learn how to support her when she had a fit, thus providing her with more opportunities for learning. Through sending her home, the school disabled her further, because staff and pupils came to view Madge as different.

Gradually, Madge started to find learning at school more and more difficult and, when she was ten years old, her doctor advised her parents to send her to a boarding school for children with learning difficulties. In the spring of 1960, Madge started this boarding school in Surrey.

For Madge, this was a major watershed, separating her from her 'ordinary' life. The boarding school was situated in the grounds of a hospital, and was clearly segregated from the outside community. As a consequence of isolating people with learning difficulties, they are denied access to many social and educational facilities, regardless of their potential abilities.

Madge said that she enjoyed the school and she did very well there, receiving many certificates as one of the top achievers. Nevertheless, it could be argued that, if her previous school had provided appropriate support, she could have stayed within her home community and not needed to change school. Madge came home only during the holiday periods. Her family visited her every other weekend, and took her out on day trips, visiting various places.

Madge finished school when she was 16 years old. She had the choice of going to 'a big place' for adults with learning difficulties, which I assume to be an institution, to which a lot of students from her school went. However, her family did not want her to go because of the distance from her home: they could not stand the prospect of not seeing her for long periods, and so she came back home instead.

Much as Madge liked school, she was very happy to be back home. Conventionally, the expectation is that school leavers choose a career, set goals and aim for them. Some people go on to further education, others get jobs, but Madge did not have those choices; no one asked her what she wanted to do. Everyone, including Madge herself, believed that it was best for her to go to an adult training centre for people with learning difficulties.

She started at the Centre two weeks after she finished school. It was a sheltered workplace where she was measuring and cutting material for electric blankets and paid £1.00 every two weeks. Even at the time, this was a ridiculously low rate of pay. Even though she saved her wages, Madge found that every time she wanted to buy something she had to ask her parents for money. She worked but she did not have money to buy things for herself. This is less likely to be the case for people without learning difficulties. Normally if people work, their pay is expected to reflect the amount of work they do. So, by paying people with learning disabilities low wages we are in fact teaching them how to remain dependent. Nevertheless, Madge enjoyed her work and made a lot of friends. Her parents were very supportive to the training centre: they offered a mini-bus and drove it for the people who attended the centre.

In 1969 Madge's eldest brother, John, was married; her second brother, Peter, was married two years later. Originally, it was planned that Madge would be a bridesmaid at John's wedding, but her father intervened, saying: 'No, you need to wait your turn.' Madge has never been sure what he meant by that, but she was not a bridesmaid even though she says that she really wanted to be one.

Madge was old enough at that time to make her own decisions, and, if her father had a good reason for not allowing her to be a bridesmaid, he should have explained clearly. Although Madge enjoyed attending both of these wedding ceremonies, she missed a valuable experience, in all likelihood because of her disability.

Madge said at this point in the narrative that she had never thought about herself getting married or having children, even when her brothers, cousins and friends got married and started families. In 1972, Madge and her parents moved house to another village within Hampshire and, as a result, Madge had to change training centres. She says that she did not mind this, but she did not have any choice at all in selecting her own workplace, another example of her being denied equality of opportunity which would be offered to non-learning-disabled people.

Madge started at a day service which was situated in the grounds of a hospital, and where she did the same work that she did at the adult training centre (measuring and cutting materials for electric blankets). However, she did not get paid for this work at all. A year after she started attending the day service, it was decided to stop offering the sheltered work and to provide leisure aspects for the service users instead. Madge had craft and needle-work classes five days a week. She found them boring after a while, but she did not know how to complain about it. The service users occasionally went out, but only to a local shop about a five-minute walk from the day service. Eventually, the service started to introduce other classes and to use some other local facilities: Madge began attending a further education college to do cooking and needlework.

In 1977, just before Christmas, a tragic accident happened. Madge was at a Christmas party organised by a social club for people with learning difficulties. Her parents had a car accident while they were on their way to a hospital to collect tablets for Madge's epilepsy. One of the staff took her to the hospital, but did not tell her why she was going there. She was left sitting in a waiting room for a long time with no idea why she was there. Madge was 27 years old at this time, and she was more than capable of understanding the situation if someone had taken the time to explain it to her. After a couple of hours, her brother Peter arrived and was told what had happened. Madge's father died in the accident and her mother damaged her back and legs. Madge was upset and cried and, while her mother was in hospital, Madge stayed in Peter's house.

When Madge was telling me of this tragic incident, she kept saying:

> Someone could have told me earlier why I was waiting at
> the hospital.

The Declaration of Rights of Mentally Retarded Persons (1971) states that: 'the mentally retarded person has to the maximum degree of feasibility the same rights as other human beings'. Madge had a right to know what had happened as soon as possible.

The year 1981 proved to be a wonderful and adventurous time for Madge. She went to Australia with her mother to visit their relatives. They spent eight weeks there, mainly in Sydney. When they decided to go there, her doctor advised her mother not to take a direct flight and to have a one-night stopover in Singapore because he believed that a long flight would make Madge too tired. However, Madge herself decided that she would be fine to take the direct flight. It took 24 hours and Madge was tired, but she did not have any significant problems and enjoyed the flight. In Australia they visited a lot of places and tried various kinds of food. Madge had a great time there. She says:

I wanted to stay there longer. I want to go there again!

This must have been a valuable opportunity for her: not many people had visited Australia by the early 1980s, and certainly not many people with learning difficulties.

At the beginning of 1993 Madge was told by her social worker that there was an option to leave home and live in a group home with other people. She decided that she wanted to try this experience and her social worker took her there. It was agreed that she would live there for a month as a trial period.

Madge moved into the house in March 1993. She tried one month then she decided that she liked it there and wanted to live there permanently. Her mother was not very happy with her decision because she already missed Madge a lot, even though she came back home almost every weekend. However, Madge's mother did not try to change the decision and she agreed happily for her daughter.

From the first day Madge moved into this group home she started to look after her own money. One year later she started to take care of all her tablets. By moving out from her parents' house into the group home, she very quickly gained more independence, wider choice and a greater responsibility for her life. After Madge moved into the group home, she decided to go to the day service twice a week and to try different things offered by the house or other organisations. Eventually she started to go to the day service only on Thursdays and, in October 1996, Madge finally decided not to go to the day service any more: she felt that she had been there too long and wanted to try different things.

Figure 7.1 Lifemap – Madge

She has recently participated in a course at a local university college, on which the college students and people with learning difficulties spend one day a week together doing things they like and things they have wanted to try. This course is held for ten weeks each year. Madge has taken part in this programme twice (in 1993 and 1994), and the aspect which she most enjoyed was visiting the Tower of London.

Currently, Madge has quite a busy life. She attends various classes (e.g. social skills, cooking, computers, etc.) during the week, and goes home every weekend. On Wednesday evenings, she normally goes to the 'CauseWay Club' run by the Baptist Church.

However, all her activities are for people with learning difficulties; she does not have opportunities to join activities or classes for people without learning difficulties. Nevertheless, her house has a lot of visitors, including volunteers, students from the college, residents' families and friends, and Madge goes out with them from time to time. Madge takes responsibility for her own money, so she can save up to buy whatever she wants, just like the rest of the population can do.

Throughout Madge's life as a whole, she has had a only couple of valuable opportunities and chances to mix with people without learning difficulties; these opportunities have been limited by her parents, doctors and other professionals. She has been dependent on her parents, and especially on her mother, throughout her entire life.

Since Madge decided to move into the group home where she currently lives, she has been making her own decisions on almost everything with support from her mother and the staff, especially her key worker. Madge feels that she is more independent now, but she has missed a lot of opportunities in life, notably the choice of continuing in mainstream education, getting a job and forming a lasting relationship with a boyfriend.

8

Tim

I first met Tim in July 1996 when I started working as an agency nurse at his home. He always seemed rather troubled and out of place there, but I got on well with him and every time I went to his home he was always happy to see me. He would shake my hand and have a broad smile on his face. When I started my case-study module, I had already decided, that with Tim's permission, I would like him to be its subject. I first raised the possibility of his involvement in November 1996, when a trusted care assistant with whom Tim got on well organised for us to get together and have a chat. I explained to Tim what I was doing and asked whether he would be willing to help me and participate in my project. He immediately agreed and, soon after this meeting, I wrote Tim a letter to formalise our arrangement. He is able to read a little bit, and I was confident that, if he had any problems, he would feel happy to ask his key worker, Tony, for help.

I did not receive a reply to my letter and felt it was necessary to contact Tim again to check that he had received it. I met him in January, he confirmed that he had received the letter and was still happy to go ahead with the project. His consent led to various discussions with the home manager and Tim's key worker about the issues of confidentiality and anonymity, in which I was able to reassure them that Tim's confidentiality and that of the home would be maintained. There were also concerns that issues of some sensitivity might arise, as this has happened in the past. I was made aware that Tim had experienced some form of abuse when he was younger, some 20 years or more ago, and that an investigation into this abuse was currently underway. Both the home manager and Tim's key worker felt that it might be necessary to have a trusted employee close by to assist if necessary if a situation became sensitive. I agreed to this and explained that I did not want in any way to cause any distress to Tim, and that any support mechanisms that were in place would be welcomed by me. They also asked that the final copies of any form of audio recording of our meetings should be destroyed on completion of the project. Again I agreed to this without question.

My meetings with Tim took place on a very casual, *ad-hoc* basis. I was also given access to his case notes by the manager of the home, which contained very factual, impersonal information about Tim, which did not really reflect his life history. There were a great number of gaps in the case file, with many unexplained details of his whereabouts.

Tim is easily distracted and finds it difficult to sit and talk for more than ten to fifteen minutes at a time, and so I felt our time together would be better spent in a casual way and chatting about things when they came up rather than creating a false situation for him to talk. It is important to point out that Tim is a very able person, who maintains his own personal care and is able to prepare simple meals with verbal assistance. He keeps himself occupied with his radio and TV and will take himself off to bed when he is tired. He is able to use the telephone independently to call his brother and has no problem making requests or making himself understood. Tim has suffered from mental illness in the past which has been controlled using medication, although he requires the medication less now.

Tim was born in a small, sleepy, picturesque village in the South of England. His memories of his home are very happy although somewhat imprecise. He enjoys making people aware of his roots and talks of his home with a sense of pride mixed with an air of regret that he no longer lives there. He is always keen to tell new people where he comes from and to encourage them to visit there if they have not already done so.

He is the youngest of three children, and was born in 1955. He has a brother called Angus, who is soon to be married, and whom Tim greatly admires. The two brothers are in regular contact, and Tim has a weekly ritual of phoning Angus on Monday, Wednesday and Friday evenings. This ritual is very important for Tim and seems to give him a sense of well-being and security. The time at which his phone call is made is often at the discretion of the members of staff on duty and Tim gets quite agitated at this time, especially if he has asked several times and is repeatedly told to wait a while longer. Tim also makes regular visits to the home of his brother at weekends, although not every weekend as Tim would wish.

Tim also has a sister called Sonia and a niece called Sophie with whom he talks occasionally on the phone, but otherwise has little contact with except at Christmas. Tim feels passionately about them, and even when he is just talking about them he is filled with a sense of visible pride and his face lights up. He told me about Sophie's birthday celebrations, although he was not sure exactly how old she is, and of how happy it makes him to see them on his visits. Sometimes, when he phones his brother Angus, his sister is there also which means he gets the chance to talk to her at these times as well.

Tim's mother now lives in a nursing home, and, again, he says he sees very little of her although he knows where she lives. He sees her about once in every six months and seems dismayed at this, wishing he could see her more often. It was not clear to me why he was not able to see her more, and Tim himself did not really seem to know the reason. His father is dead, and Tim expresses his understanding of that concept by saying that his father 'has popped off to heaven'.

Tim has lived in his current home, a nursing home for adults with learning disabilities, for 18 months. As is often the case, Tim appears to have had little choice in the move and this placement seems to have been all that was made available to him. He was unable to explain the reason for the move, or even where he came from, except to call it 'home', by which he could have meant the place where he lived with his mother. He often refers to his home now as the prison, but he treats it more like a hotel and he does not like helping in any of its domestic activities. He is often asked and will help with some persuasion.

The kitchen in the home is accessible only to members of staff and so Tim is unable to make himself a drink or anything to eat and has to ask permission if he wants anything outside of meal times. At the moment he and some of the other residents of the home are in temporary accommodation while renovation work is being carried out on their home. He much prefers living in the temporary accommodation, and would rather stay here than return to his own home.

It is sometimes difficult for Tim to recall past events. Remembering places and hospitals where he had lived proved particularly hard, and he preferred not to talk about that, saying he did not like it there and it made him sad. I read in his case-notes that he had been sectioned under the mental health act on two occasions and spent some three or more years in custodial care in hospitals under that act. When I asked him about one of the hospitals, at first he denied he had ever lived there and then changed his mind and said he had, and that he had not liked it at all. It is obviously an issue of great sadness and pain for him and I did not want to pursue it so we decided not to talk about it anymore. This made Tim a lot happier.

We moved on to talk about some happy times Tim has had in his life. His religion by birth is Church of England, although he does not attend church now and says he does not like it. The ordinary activities of life seem quite limited for Tim with very few choices available to him. He would like to go out a lot more in the community and to socialise, but, again, with the constraints of his life in the home, including the availability of staffing, money and the lack of freedom to come and go as he pleases, it is often not possible for him to do as he wishes. In the home itself, there is an acute awareness of responsibility for the safety of all the residents, and a secure lock system is used, whereby residents must be accompanied by a member of staff on trips outside.

Tim attends a day centre four days a week and mainly participates in craft activities, which he finds quite boring. He recently began going to the local college one day a week where he is learning to read and write and improve the skills he already has. This he really enjoys and he would like to go more often. There is to be a meeting about the possibility of extending his time at college, but Tim himself will not be present. It will be between the college staff and Tim's key worker.

Tim is very independent in taking care of himself, yet his life in the nursing home seems at odds with his abilities. Very few of his fellow residents are able to have a conversation with him, which he finds quite frustrating, and his only other source of chat is the staff. However, Tim prefers to spend most of his time alone in his own room, listening to his radio or watching his television.

Tim talked about some of the good things in his life. He recalled one of his happiest memories was the middle school he attended as a child. In particular, one of his teachers, Mr Winton, made him very happy there. He enjoyed going to the school and learning there. He also likes sports, especially volleyball, and, although he has never been to see a football match, he would like to see one one day. Tim said, for him, his favourite hobby is eating, especially fish and chips on Fridays and cheese sandwiches for his supper. He also enjoys spending time going to the pub and having a beer, although this is not something he does often because it is dependent on the staff on duty in the home.

Tim likes women a lot. He is very friendly and attempts to be openly affectionate to people he likes. Some of the female staff at his home find this very difficult to cope with, and Tim is often discouraged from demonstrating this behaviour. Tim has never had a girlfriend but would like one very much. At 42 years of age, he seems quite a lonely person.

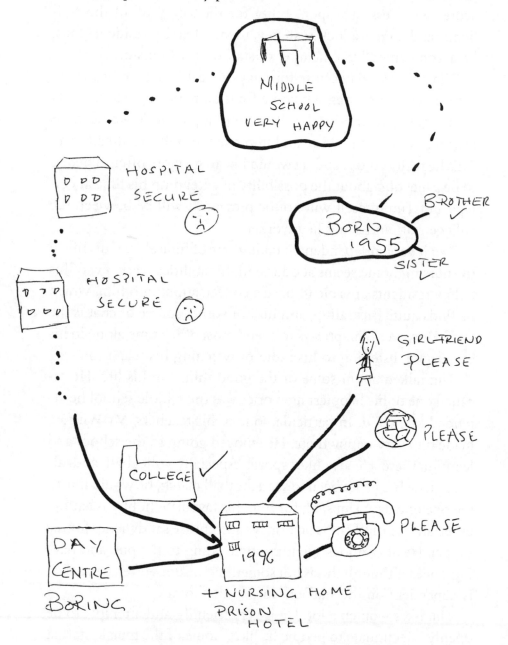

Figure 8.1 Lifemap – Tim

9

Colin

This is the story of Colin's life, as he remembers it. In my opinion, Colin genuinely welcomed the opportunity to look back at his life as well as gaining from the social aspect of the research process. We met on several occasions, both at his home and at a local cafe, to spend time talking about his memories. In a final meeting at his home, we taped our conversation and wrote his life history on a large piece of paper, with smiling faces and unhappy faces to denote the happy and sad points in his life. We made use of pictures to aid Colin's understanding of what was written on the paper, although I felt that it would be inappropriate to submit this material with the written record, because it was exceptionally personal to Colin. I have therefore, written his story in my own words, supported by quotations from Colin taken from the taped conversation.

Colin was born in Hampshire in 1960. He has Down's syndrome and moderate learning disabilities. He could not tell me when he was born, but he knew his age and so we were able to work out the year of birth. He lived with his parents in a small village in Hampshire and has only vague memories of his childhood and of living with his parents. He has a younger brother with whom he remains in contact with and sees on a regular basis, but Colin seems to have no earlier memories of time spent with this brother.

Colin attended two local special schools in Hampshire, of which he seems to have no memories, other than their names.

While he was at the second school Colin's father died, and, with help from the staff, we calculated that this must have happened some time around 1976. Colin remembers this event, because it appears to coincide with the time that he moved out of home to go to a large residential institution about 20 miles away from mum:

> Yeah my dad passed away and I had to move away from my mum … lived in big house. Mum came to see me sometimes.

Colin talks about a large house and big long rooms, and he gets angry and upset when he talks about his time there. Residents at the home all slept in large dormitories with nowhere to put personal belongings, and little or no chance of any privacy. He certainly made it obvious that he did not enjoy his time spent there:

> Horrible, it was horrible we were all in long rooms it was like a hospital ward and there were so many people. Yeah, people everywhere just wandering around. Not never going back.

When we talked about this topic he became noticeably agitated, so the conversation changed to talking about his life in his new home. In 1987 Colin moved to a small group home with five other residents, located near to his family home. There, Colin was encouraged to be more independent and to make choices about his life. He appears to have much clearer memories from this point and talks more freely about all the activities that he participates in:

> I do lots of things, I go to watch football matches and do cookery and I got a job that I chose yeah working in a cafe made lot of friends.

Colin finds it hard to talk in any chronological order about life experiences he has encountered, but he talks quite freely about all the things in which he has participated, including adult education, work and an active social life.

Colin has taken a variety of adult education classes including courses in computing, art and, at present, a cookery course:

> Yeah I'm doing cookery yeah at ———— school it is up the road. I enjoy it, we made biscuits and I help to cook the tea at home I do.

Sometime around 1993/94 Colin got his first job working as a cleaner in a children's home. However, this information came only from the staff, as Colin himself seems to have no memory of this work. He does, however, remember his second job, working in a public house, mainly doing washing up duties:

> I liked the pub until new person come and say they don't need me any more.

From what I can gather, the pub changed hands and was closed for refurbishment, during which time the manager decided that he no longer required Colin's services.

Unfortunately, in addition to losing his job, Colin also lost his mother at the beginning of 1995 which, according to staff, he took very badly. In the summer of that year, the staff recommended that Colin should have an advocate to help him cope with his bereavement: it was in this role that I first met Colin in September 1995. We talked through his feelings about his mother and I encouraged him to visit her grave:

> I miss my mum. I go to put flowers on the grave. I went with M at Easter to put flower there.

At the end of 1995, Colin became one of a group of volunteers responsible for helping with the upkeep of a local steam railway. He talks about this enthusiastically, and, from what I can gather from him, he cleans the trains and the stations and even does some painting:

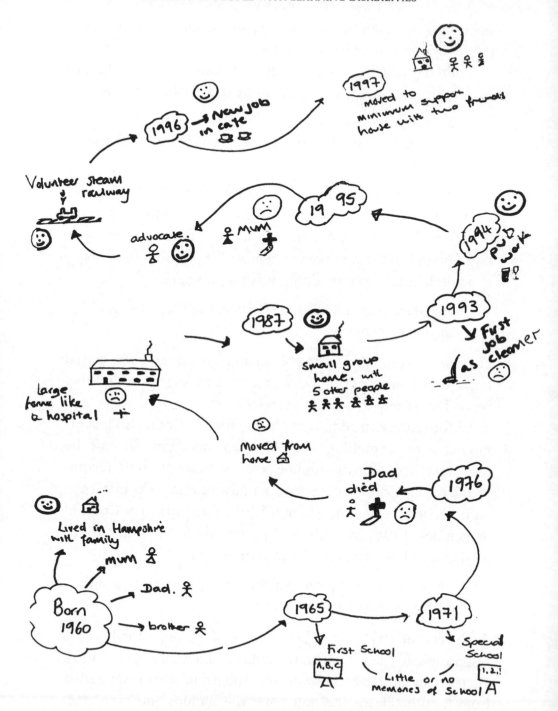

Figure 9.1 Lifemap – Colin

> Yeah the W line every Friday. I like it and we get to wear overalls and a bright yellow vest, yeah bright yellow we wear. We are working at ———— station.

Colin recently began a new job working one day a week in a cafe. His duties include washing up and clearing tables. He does not get paid, but he gets a free lunch when he has finished his shift. He has made a lot of friends at this job, and enjoys going out to lunch there on his days off:

> Yeah I work there on a Wednesday I see N he's my boss and K he helps me. I like working there and K helps me in the kitchen and I get dinner, nice food. I'm not working this week 'cos it's Easter but I go on Wednesdays.

Colin enjoys his life at the moment and also talks enthusiastically about several other activities that he participates in, including swimming, going to a sports club, regularly going to church and watching professional football. It is my judgement that Colin leads a full and varied life and he is very happy:

> I go to watch football and I collect programmes yeah J takes me, I got three programmes now. I go swimming on Friday night and I go to the bar for a drink too, sometimes I eat there. Yeah burger and chips.

10

Sue

This is the story of lady who has not always had learning difficulties, but, as a result of an accident at the age of nine in which she was knocked down by a car, subsequently suffered brain damage as well as epilepsy. Ever since this event she has had to go to special schools and colleges specifically for those who have learning difficulties.

Sue's story begins in 1961 when she was born in Fife in Scotland. This was quite a small and friendly town, where she lived with her mother, father, older brother and younger sister. Sue's earliest memories of this time were playing with her older brother climbing trees and other things. This, she explained, was because she was a 'tomboy' and preferred boys' games to playing with her dolls. Unfortunately, this got her into a bit of trouble as she explains:

> I remember when I was three walking along a wall that was ten feet high, and then falling off.

When asked how she did it and whether she hurt herself, she replied:

> it was easy: I just stepped off the wall and down I fell. No I did not hurt myself much, only a few scratches.

Also at this time she started primary school within the village; this, she said was a very happy time which she enjoyed immensely, as she started to read and write.

In 1967, when Sue was six almost seven, the family moved down to Essex in England, where her father had a new job. Here Sue again attended a mainstream primary school, where, again, she enjoyed all the lessons, especially reading and writing stories. The fact that Sue can read and write is still a real source of pride and enjoyment to her.

She attended this school in Essex with her younger sister for the next three years until 1970, which was to be the most significant year in Sue's early life. This was the year she was knocked over by a motor car, fracturing her skull and later being diagnosed as having received brain damage resulting from the accident. Unsurprisingly, this caused everyone a great deal of anxiety and pain.

After Sue's injuries had healed sufficiently enough for her to return to school, it was decided that she would not return to the school where she had previously been, but transfer to a special school in the same town. According to Sue this was a time that she hated as she did not like this place at all. One reason for her change in attitude was that the boys did all the things that she wanted to do, but, at this school, girls were not allowed to join in with 'boyish' activities. Furthermore, at her other school, Sue had enjoyed spending quiet times reading alone and this was difficult to do in her new environment.

Sue became frustrated at her new school and, consequently, found it hard to fit in with any of her peer group, became isolated and a target for bullying from both the boys and girls. When we talked about this she said that she was bullied a lot of the time. During the telling of her story Sue said:

> I hated going to the ESN schools because I was treated differently from the school I went to before.

In November 1976 Sue went to a new school which was again a segregated school, and at which all the pupils were younger than herself, which she found very upsetting. She began to fight with the other pupils because she found the school very loud and noisy, which she hated. Sue was at this school for five years, not really enjoying this time and feeling very upset and angry because all those around her were younger and so she felt that she did not really fit in. She became increasingly aggressive towards the other students if they annoyed her.

Eventually, in 1981, while Sue was moving again to another residential college, her parents moved back to Scotland. This was very hard for her, as she was again feeling uneasy about moving to a new place herself and the fact that her parents were so far away made it very difficult for her to accept the changes in her life.

The college, where she still lives, was very different from the other places that she had been. Apart from her time in Scotland, Sue had always been in larger towns, but here she was in the heart of the countryside, totally isolated from friends and family, in a strange place where she had not been before. She said that before her parents left, after bringing her to the college, they said she would have to grin and bear it as there was nowhere else for her to go. This comment, possibly meant as encouragement by her parents who were feeling as unsure as Sue herself, added to her feelings of helplessness and frustration.

During the conversation about her life in which she had been forthcoming and clear, Sue mentioned something which did not seem consistent with the opinion I was forming of her. She said:

> I cannot communicate with people but I am supposed to forget about all that now.

This seemed a bizarre statement, since Sue and I had spent at least two hours talking about things, and she seemed to be very articulate in communicating what she wanted to say. From her attitude throughout our time spent together and from other things she said it would seem that, at some stage, Sue has been told that she has communication problems. This comment, made some time in the past, has obviously caused resentment and is an example of the careless and often thoughtless comments made to Sue by people around her who may have thought she was not able to understand. Sue obviously does understand much if not all of what is said to her, and remarks such as this have served only to add to her frustration over the years.

Here in her new home she found that, at 20 years of age, she was again the oldest person, and this gave rise to the same old problems. A lot of the others, especially the men in the college, liked to play loud music and were themselves very loud and boisterous. Consequently the same feelings of frustration and resentment built up as before.

One factor that was better at the new home was that Sue felt very much more able to look after herself and through this became more independent. For the next three years things progressed with Sue not really enjoying the fact that she was the oldest, but at least feeling that she was able to do some things that she had not been able to experience before. She gradually became more independent which pleased her as she did not have to rely on others for all her needs.

Another issue that emerged from our conversation about her life was that she does not like to be told what to do and when to do things. Sue said she liked to go on holiday but would rather make up her own mind when she wanted to go rather than be told when and where and have no say in the matter.

One issue that has come up throughout this story of Sue's life is the fact that, since her accident, she has been in schools and colleges where she is always the oldest by a large margin and this has caused her a great deal of anxiety. While I was talking to her, I learned that, in a short while, she was to move away from the college into a small group home in Yorkshire with people of her own age. This, Sue told me, was one of the best things to happen to her in a long time and she could hardly wait for the time to come when she would move there permanently.

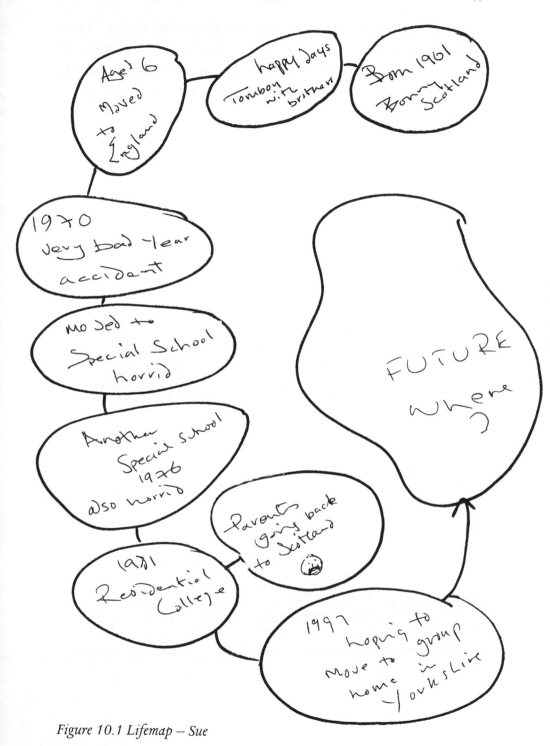

Figure 10.1 Lifemap – Sue

As a postscript, I must add that, at the time of writing up Sue's story, I heard that she has moved to Yorkshire, is really enjoying her new life there and has also found a few hours' voluntary work in a garden centre, something which she never had while at the college.

11

Jane

Jane was born at her family home in July 1966, the sixth addition to the family. She now has seven brothers and two sisters, with all of whom she shares a close and loving relationship. Jane still lives at home with her mother and father, although all of her siblings have left the family home and now have partners and families of their own. She has regular contact with all of her brothers and sisters, and has travelled to California to see one of her brothers.

Jane grew up in large Wiltshire town where she attended the local playgroup until the age of five, transferring then to a newly opened special needs school, having been diagnosed as having special needs. The school catered for children between the ages of two and nineteen. Jane continued her education there, was very happy and had many friends, including one particular best friend, Mary, whom she remembers fondly. Jane has many photographs of their time together, but has no contact with her now. Jane enjoyed school and was very interested in reading and writing, an area that she is pursuing at present through adult evening classes at a local further education college. She also enjoyed sports, especially running, which helped her keep her weight under control, as she has a tendency to put it on easily. Now, however, Jane is very health conscious about what she eats:

> I don't diet just eat healthy foods like salad … I don't want to run again!

Jane told me that she was never really naughty at school but that she did like to do things in her own way:

> It's all right when people ask you to do something … teachers just tell you what to do!

Jane reminisced happily about her childhood, remembering how she always enjoyed playing with the boys more than the girls, particularly her elder brother's friends: Jane was known as a bit of a 'tomboy' by her family and close friends and she still keeps her hair as short as she did as a child, even though her mum tried to encourage her to grow it!

When Jane was approximately ten years of age, her mother and father fostered a young boy with severe learning disabilities, who spent three years with the family. Jane built a very close relationship with Paul and was able to enhance both his communication skills and walking ability, because of the length of time she spent playing with him, giving him encouragement. Jane and her family have always remained in contact with Paul and have regular letters and photographs from him. Jane has very fond memories of Paul and is eager to see him again, which she hopes to do over the summer.

One of Jane's most vivid memories from her childhood was the death of her nan with whom she had had a very close relationship and whom she saw every day, as she lived just down the road:

> I used to visit Nan a lot but she's dead now … I was sad, I still miss her sometimes.

It is evident that Jane had a very happy and fulfilling childhood, surrounded by a large family and many friends, and that she does not recall any really unhappy times apart from the death of her nan.

When Jane left school at the age of 19, she did not go on to further education or employment but attended a local day centre. She did not enjoy her time there and was glad to leave when her family moved to Wales two years later. Upon moving to Wales, it was discovered that Jane had a hole in her heart and needed surgery. The operation was carried out at the Hammersmith hospital in London and Jane can recall very vividly her time in hospital and speaks of the doctors and her consultant:

> He was very nice!

Jane also remembered both her parents and one of her brothers being at the hospital when she woke from her operation, and still has a video made by her friends at her local club wishing her well. Jane further commented that she now has to take two tablets a day:

> To stop any problems with my heart, but it should be all right now.

While Jane was living in Wales she attended another day centre, although this one was rather different from the one in Wiltshire and was not called a day centre at all, but rather the ———— Club:

> It was great at the club we went shopping out for lunch …
> We could do loads more stuff, trips, I went to Minorca …
> We had a sewing club … I could see loads of people, had more friendly friends and people use to phone me up all the time, it was better than the day centre.

Jane made many friends while she was in Wales she still sees them twice a year and keeps in regular contact by the telephone and through letters.

At the age of 26 Jane moved with her parents to the small Berkshire town where she is currently living, and enrolled at a local college of further education which she really enjoyed. Unfortunately, after finishing the course, Jane could not find a job and now attends the local day centre, with which she is not impressed:

> I wanted to go for a little while, it's all right … I preferred the one in Wales, more friendly people. This one's not as

nice … I've only got a few friends at the day centre – I don't get on very well with them sometimes.

At present, Jane works on two practical work experience placements which were set up by the day centre, one of which she very much enjoys as a helper at a parent and toddler group. This is an area that, if she had a choice, she would like to pursue further, although she does say that she would not want to work every day. She was less enthusiastic about her other work experience placement which is working in an old people's home. Nevertheless, she did comment:

I don't mind it sometimes, old people need help … I wouldn't like to do it all the time.

She also takes part in a sheltered work scheme which she very much enjoys, not least because she is paid £2.00 a day for her work.

At present, Jane has a variety of interests and quite a busy social life: she goes swimming on a Tuesday, Gateway Club on a Wednesday, adult evening classes on a Thursday and visits friends on a Saturday for lunch. She has not found very much to do in her home town apart from going shopping with her mum, who pays for her clothes although Jane chooses them. Jane does have her own bank account but her mum collects her benefits for her. She enjoys listening to a variety of music, watching *EastEnders* and a television cookery programme on which she would like to appear.

In the future, Jane believes that she does not want to get married:

I had a boyfriend but I've given up on boys for a while … I don't want to get married.

She added, however, that she does sometimes get lonely at home and would like another foster brother or sister. The prospect of

Day Centre not happy

21yn old went to Wales with Mum + dad

heart operation

another Day Centre and club — very good ☺

26 yrs old

back to England Berks. with Mum + Dad

1966 Born Wilts 7 brothers 2 sisters

Parents foster younger brother with learning difficulties

liked school especially sport/running

same school until 19 yr old

at 5 → Special School

play group

going to local College
learning reading & writing
having some work experience
really enjoying it   £2.00 per day
pay
has own bank account
has given up on boys

all brothers & sisters left home visited them all over the world.

Figure 11.1 Lifemap – Jane

leaving home or what she would like to do in the future has never really occurred to Jane and she says:

I'll keep on going on with what I'm doing.

12

Mat

To assure anonymity for the person I interviewed for this assignment, I will use a pseudonym for the person being described: I shall call him Mat.

The interview was carried out at Mat's home in Hampshire, with his parents present. He thought this would be better for me, just in case he was not able to remember particular incidents in his life, where his parents might help him out. I made sure to listen very carefully to Mat, and to direct the questions to him and not his parents. I felt this would allow me to get as accurate an insight as possible into his life, rather than his parents' interpretation of that life.

Before I undertook the interview, I sent Mat a letter telling him exactly what I was hoping to achieve and I followed this up with a phone call a week later. Mat agreed to meet me at his house, and we came to the view that only one interview would take place because of the timescale placed on the assignment. The interview itself lasted one and a half hours and generated the life history which follows.

Mat was born in October 1974 in the general hospital of a large city; he has lived with his parents all his life in Hampshire. They told me that they felt that, when he was young, he was institutionalised by the doctors to get him out of the way, which made them very angry. But this situation altered when they met a professor of paediatrics who had helped change attitudes towards people like Mat. He introduced him to physiotherapy and speech therapy, from which Mat's parents believed that he benefited. However, they emphasise that in the late 1970s and early 1980s, there were few therapists, and that those who were available were very expensive. For example, in the first four to five years of his life, Mat visited a speech therapist, but, when he was seven, the therapy had to stop for financial reasons. As a result, his parents feel that Mat has developed a stutter whereas, had the therapy continued, his speech would have been much improved.

When Mat was two and a half, he went two or three mornings a week to a special school for children with severe learning disabilities. Within that time he also went to a mainstream playgroup, run by the Royal Navy. His parents felt that Mat benefited from this, particularly as there was a good ratio of staff to children – one member of staff to six children. Mat has little recollection of this, so his parents advocated for him.

Mat stayed at this same school until he was 16, although he had had a pre-school assessment at the age of four. His parents believe that he would have been capable enough to attend a mainstream school, but was not offered the opportunity. They feel that the headteacher of the local mainstream school was reluctant to take on a child with Mat's needs, and truly feel her to have been prejudiced.

At the age of 13, while still at school, Mat started at a local college one day a week where he learned basic and life skills such as cooking, art and craft. Mat said he enjoyed it there, because he could mix with mainstream students. At 16, Mat went to a unit attached to a hospital. He went there every day, participated in activities such as writing work, cooking, recreation, playing cards, reading, listening to music and acquiring general skills. Throughout the week, he would also go to a mainstream college, where he would do some computer work. Again, Mat liked the college as once more he was given the opportunity to mix with mainstream students. While at the unit, he made some good friends, and received positive support. Of the eight users who attended, each had individual one-to-one support. Mat also attended the drama club there, taking part in a drama festival doing a performance of mime. He particularly remembers this, as he received a special award, in the form of a big cup. Mat added this trophy to the gold medal which he won in a disabled swimming competition while he was at school.

When Mat turned 19, problems began to arise. The unit decided that it could not accommodate him any longer, giving financial difficulties as the reason. This resulted in a battle between Mat's parents and the education authority. Many letters were exchanged and Mat was finally allowed to stay where he was for his final academic year. However, Mat remembers feeling very rejected and isolated at this time.

Just before Mat turned 20, he went to the special needs department of the local mainstream college as a full-time student. He was extremely thrilled about this opportunity as he was going to mix with mainstream students and make new friends. Mat's parents also expressed their delight, particularly as previous schools did not provide any opportunities to participate in any kind of sport, whereas at this college there was a timetabled sport afternoon, which gave Mat the chance to sample a range of sporting activities. Mat remembers this and says he had enjoyed it.

Mat's parents also make the point that, at previous schools, there was a high percentage of female staff and not enough male members of staff. They feel this has led Mat to miss out on a lot of male bonding, and Mat agrees with this.

He also specifically remembers lunchtimes at the college – pizza and Diet Coke which he said he really enjoyed as it was his choice, and he was given his own money to spend. He also remembers playing football at college and scoring a goal, which seemed to give him a great sense of fulfilment and reward.

When he was at college his parents remember the particular problems they faced when the students went on work experience, as there didn't seem to be anything available for Mat. One

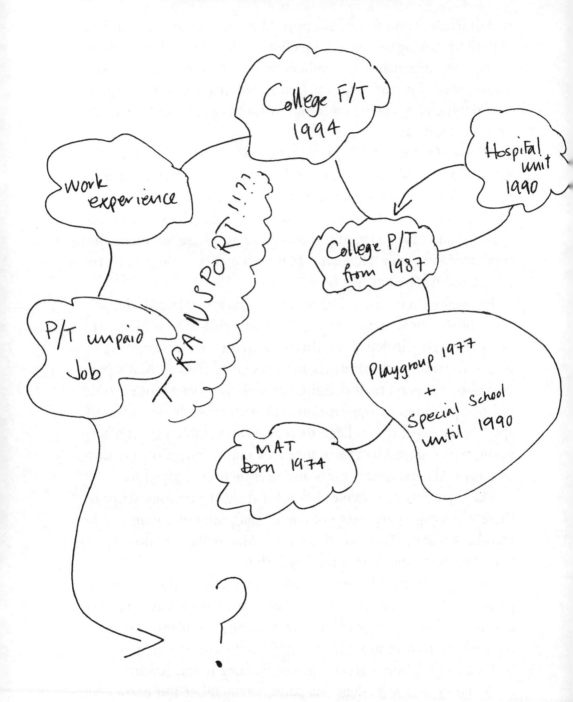

Figure 12.1 Lifemap – Mat

gardening placement said that they would accept Mat but then changed their minds, after originally saying they would willingly accept anyone with a disability. He then found another placement with another gardening business and really enjoyed it there, even growing his own vegetables which his mum and dad used for dinner.

As he did really well at the gardening company, he wanted to go back there after he finished college. At 21, it was arranged that he would work for the company for three days a week, attending college for the other two days. Mat was extremely happy and excited about starting there, even though he was not being paid. However, his parents remember the problems they still had with respect to transport. Neither the education authority nor the health authority was prepared to pay for Mat's transport to work, on the grounds that he was still attending college. Eventually, social services proved extremely helpful in solving the problem, but Mat's parents still believe that the situation could have been resolved much earlier if the authorities had used a bit of common sense and ignored the bureaucracy.

The transport issue was a major factor in determining whether Mat could go to work or not, and Mat remembers being very upset about it. This was a very frustrating and worrying time for whole the family, who feel that it demonstrates the inflexibility of the services available for people with learning disabilities. They feel that the local education authority, health authority and social services should all work together, instead of fighting over who will sign the cheque. Mat says that he likes going to the garden, but would not want to go every day, as it is hard work.

In the future, Mat says that he would ideally like to work on a farm, but his parents feel that the opportunity may not be there. In general, Mat seems to have been happy with the way his life has gone.

13

Matthew

Matthew was born in August of 1976, in a city in the south of England 'during the year of the heatwave'. His two older sisters were aged ten and fourteen at the time he was born and he recalls that he has since been told that he was 'quite a big baby'. His family lived in a small village near the city in which he was born and when he was two they moved to a different house in the same area. Matthew cannot remember much from his first few years, but said 'one of my sisters . . . she used to push, kept on wanting to push my pram'. He mentions having seen trains and stations, thus beginning an interest in railways which has grown throughout his life.

At the age of five, Matthew began attending the small, mainstream state school in the village where he lived. This was not an experience he enjoyed, finding it a 'nightmare' because the other children were too noisy and 'frightening'. His memory of mainstream schooling is of shouting teachers and frightening children, and the experience clearly did not meet his, as yet unrecognised, needs. This school 'wasn't the right school, it wasn't a special school it was an ordinary school' and so Matthew only stayed there for one year. He says of it:

> they didn't understand did they, my problem, I don't think, they didn't realise, I think that's when my parents, I think that's when they realised he had some sort of problem, me, sometimes it doesn't show, does it, 'til later years?

At the age of six, Matthew changed schools and began attending a special needs school near the city where he was born. He does not mention any process of diagnosis or assessment prior to entering segregated special needs education, nor is he clear as to when he was diagnosed as having Asperger's syndrome. At this new school, 'they were fair' and Matthew felt much more settled: he began horse riding, which he continued for the two years in which he attended this school. At this age, Matthew says he was described as 'quite a happy boy'.

Matthew next went to another special needs school, again relatively close to the village where he lived. He had his ninth birthday while at this school, and stayed there until the age of 12, the longest period at one school in his life. Again, Matthew found school problematic, describing his time there as 'a bad experience' as he encountered some difficult times. He did not wish to enlarge on what the 'not very nice things' which happened at this school were.

When he was nine, Matthew went on holiday with his family to Wales and then to the Pennines in the same year. He found that holidays with his family were enjoyable experiences. During his time at this school, Matthew met Princess Anne, and he qualifies his description of her visit by saying that 'she does a lot with special needs'. He continued horse riding, but now as an out-of-school activity with his father.

At the age of 12, Matthew changed schools yet again. He says that he applied to another school which was for boys only, but he did not get in. He moved to a special needs school in the city where he was born. This school catered for children with special needs from the age of 11 to 18 and, during his time there, he had his 14th birthday, when he recalls receiving a train set from his family. This was the beginning of a deeper interest in trains and model railways.

Matthew again describes experiencing problems at school:

There was a few problems, I might've done there, done wrong things.

These problems mainly surrounded issues of puberty and the experiencing of sexual feelings without knowing how to address them or deal with them. Matthew recalls one incident when he saw a teacher in a changing room whilst at a swimming pool, and he feels that this created a real problem for him.

Matthew's problems of making friends continued within this setting. When talking about whether he got to know people well, Matthew answers with some doubt:

I suppose I did in some ways.

When he was 15, Matthew went on holiday with his family to Cornwall. All his holidays had been taken with his family up to this point, but he then went on a holiday with his school to Malvern. The experience was overall a good one, although tinged with homesickness.

At the age of 16, Matthew graduated to the extended education unit, attached to the special school, the aim of which was to equip people for work. It was about

learning to become people, learning what work is, jobs, a home of your own, having a home of your own.

The first year in this unit was not an easy one but, by the second year it had become

easier ... 'cos I got more things to do, I could go out on my own, independently and all that.

The value of that first year eventually did become clear to Matthew, as his second year was spent actually doing the things for which he had been building up the skills in his first year. One stumbling block became apparent, however: in relation to the skills for living away from home, Matthew felt that it was not something he would be able to achieve, something which I can't get, I don't think, it's not easy for me.

Matthew recalls not being an ideal pupil:

> I remember I didn't get a driving licence application form and he [the tutor] said 'Well, you were too bone idle to come and get one!'.

When he left at the age of 18, Matthew did not keep in touch with anyone from the school, and does not see anyone from those times currently:

> No – the trouble is they've all moved on, haven't they – they've moved on doing what they like.

Matthew's next educational experience was in a further education college in a town near where he lives. This college runs courses for people with learning disabilities alongside a range of other courses. It was a different environment from that which Matthew was used to, and, additionally, the other students were, in the main, 16 as opposed to 18 like Matthew. This proved to be another negative experience in an educational setting:

> It was a very nasty place … it was really a nightmare.

The college system did not treat the students as adults:

> They treated me like a 13-year-old.

The idea was, according to Matthew, for the students to learn about 'social things', yet most of his memories are concerned with issues of being accepted. Matthew recalls:

> There was a couple of students, they were trying to be nice to me, but I kept telling them to leave me alone 'cos I knew they weren't the right ones for me.

He found it difficult to develop friendships:

> I've never had many friends … people used to be nasty to me … because they didn't understand my problem, they

had quite different sorts of needs to what I have. I think it's because I have Asperger's I have difficulties with communicating.

The year at the further education college was unrewarding and frustrating, something which Matthew tried to address by telling people he did not want to stay there. Their reaction was to say that he could 'get out', yet Matthew felt this was the setting where he found it easiest to fit in, especially among the students without special needs.

After his year at the college, Matthew began attending a small project providing a 'consumer-led' day service one day a week for adults who have a learning disability. With only four or five adults there each day, it was again a new environment. The other project users tended to be older than Matthew:

> More mature, they talk to me sensibly and give me sensible ideas.

He now has a weekly routine, spending time with support workers on Monday and Tuesday mornings, going swimming or other activities. Monday and Tuesday afternoons are spent at home. Wednesday is a 'day off', and, in the summer of 1996, Matthew began attending the project for two full days a week. In the interview, he made no mention of how these decisions were made and whether he had any level of involvement in them.

More recently, Matthew has begun attending a drama club, concerned with 'drama of communicating', practising social situations. He also has been thinking of doing something else, perhaps 'joining some sort of Gateway Club'.

Matthew makes no mention of any relationships, except to say he does not have a girlfriend.

In terms of his future, Matthew sees barriers to many things he would like to do. His idea of becoming a lorry driver is not feasible because of 'not being able to get a driving licence'. Driving is

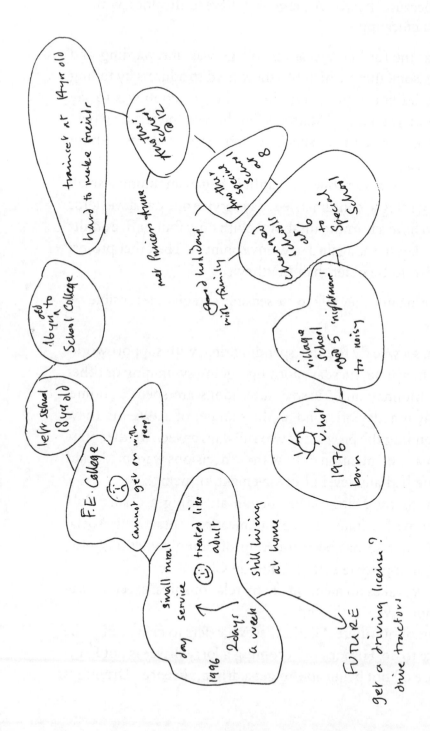

Figure 13.1 Lifemap – Matthew

something he has always thought of as being a good job, involving an interest of his:

> I've always liked driving tractors and combines and things 'cos I'm a man.

In terms of money, Matthew has a weekly allowance, 'like a benefit' but does not think of himself as 'good at money'. He does not see himself moving out of home in the near future:

> Not yet it looks like. I wish I could though because it feels like I'd be more of an adult then.

14

Michael

Michael is a lively young man who was born in 1980 and lived with his mother, father and two sisters until he was 11 years old.

In 1991 he was admitted to the care of a children's home for children with learning difficulties. This was at the request of his parents, as his father had suffered a nervous breakdown and felt he could no longer cope with Michael at home. Michael was originally admitted for six months, with the idea that he would be able to return to his parents after that time.

When he was admitted, his pen picture said that Michael was of average height, slim build and was a lively and cheerful little boy of a friendly and likeable nature. It stated that he had been diagnosed as having cerebral palsy. He liked playing with cars, listening to music, tapes and videos. He liked playing on a tricycle and had a favourite toy. His parents had also written that they were practising Christians and wrote, 'You may find that he wants to talk to Jesus'.

Staff at the home remember Michael when he first arrived as incredibly shy and insecure. He was very able to do most daily tasks such as dressing and feeding himself, but it took him some time to get to know the staff and feel comfortable with them. He was a very affectionate young boy, who liked cuddles: staff say he needed to feel secure.

After six months, Michael wanted to go home, but his father felt that he still could not cope: in this time, Michael had had virtually no contact with his family. His sisters wrote often, but he had only seen his parents a few times. The staff at the home had formed a good bond with Michael by now, and he seemed quite happy there, but they said that the situation was affecting him. They felt he showed this by constantly craving adult attention. One member of staff observed of Michael that 'he needed to belong'.

It was agreed that Michael would be accommodated by social services for a further two years, still with the prospect of returning to his parents' home. A detailed programme was worked out with Michael, the staff and his parents to integrate him back into the family home. Options were looked into to try to find Michael a foster home. An advert was placed but there was no response, so he had to stay where he was.

Michael and the staff at this point were still working on the programme to try and get him back home. But his family still felt that he was better off where he was, so it was arranged at the end of the two years that Michael would stay at the home until he was old enough to move on to an adult placement.

Michael was still attending the same school as he had been when he arrived. He enjoyed it very much there, but the staff were concerned about his constant striving for adult attention. His school review stated that: 'Michael gets on well with some of the other students, but only concentrates on tasks when working one to one with an adult. If he has not got the attention of an adult, he will demonstrate "silly behaviour" to get it.'

The staff at the home were finding that he was doing similar things there, and decided that it would be a good idea to move him into another house within the unit that had older male residents. This was an attempt to get him to mix more with his peers. They discussed this move with Michael and asked him if he would like to spend a few days in the house to see how he liked it. He agreed to this move and seemed to enjoy the new company.

In 1994, plans were being made to transform the unit from a children's home to a respite care unit. They were to no longer take on new full-time residents, although the current residents were to stay for as long as they needed, i.e. until they were old enough to move on to an adult placement. The home is now officially defined as a respite unit, and Michael is its only full-time resident.

He has his own large room with a toilet and a shower to give him his own privacy. Michael is now the oldest member of the home, the rest of the young people in his house being between 9 and 15 years old. Until recently he had two friends who came to the house for respite, but they have now turned 18 and have moved on to adult placements.

Michael has moved on from his school to a college that is associated with the school. He still sees one of his friends there. Over the six years that Michael has been a resident at the home, staff have seen many changes in him. They feel that he is much more confident, but is still very shy with people he does not know. The staff have worked very hard with him to promote his independence – one staff member said:

> He can now buy small items in a shop unaided, but as yet he has not the skills to walk to the shop alone.

Michael can prepare simple meals for himself and hot drinks. He has recently learned to ride a two-wheeler bicycle – a member of staff observed that:

> It was so undignified to see a 16-year-old young man riding around on a tricycle.

The staff are also encouraging Michael to collect model cars rather than play with toy cars on the floor.

Michael often asks why he cannot go home when he sees the other children doing so after a short stay. He also has a considerable interest in where staff live and who their family are, and he sometimes asks to go home with them. However, he refuses to talk about his own family. One key member of staff said that he gets all 'silly' and says 'I don't know' whenever they are mentioned.

Michael does see his family: he goes home for one weekend a month. But these visits are often cut short as his father says he cannot cope with him.

There are plans for Michael, when he reaches 18, to move to an adult residential home near his family so he will be able to see them more often. Staff are worried that he will not be able to cope very well in an adult environment, as they feel he still has a very childlike view of life and shows inappropriate behaviour towards people, such as cuddling instead of shaking hands when he meets them. They are working very hard to prepare him for an adult environment, and want to make the transition as pain free as possible. Michael himself says that he would like to be with people his own age, as he gets frustrated with being in the company of young children all of the time.

At the time of writing this paper, I believe the plans that have been made for Michael's move are going ahead and he is due to move into the home near his family shortly after his 18th birthday in 1998.

The birth of a child with learning disabilities is often associated with adverse effects on the family because of the view that looking after a child with learning disabilities can be the work of an 'ordinary childhood magnified and prolonged a hundred times' (Ryan and Thomas 1995, p.49). When Michael's father experienced a nervous breakdown, the family was placed in a position where greater assistance and alternative care was needed for Michael.

At that time, when Michael, at the age of 11, first went to the children's home, it was intended that he would stay for only six months: however, this was not to be the case. Michael has had no choice in this, and six years on he is still there. As in many situations with children, choices are made for them. However, there is usually some evidence that children under the age of 16

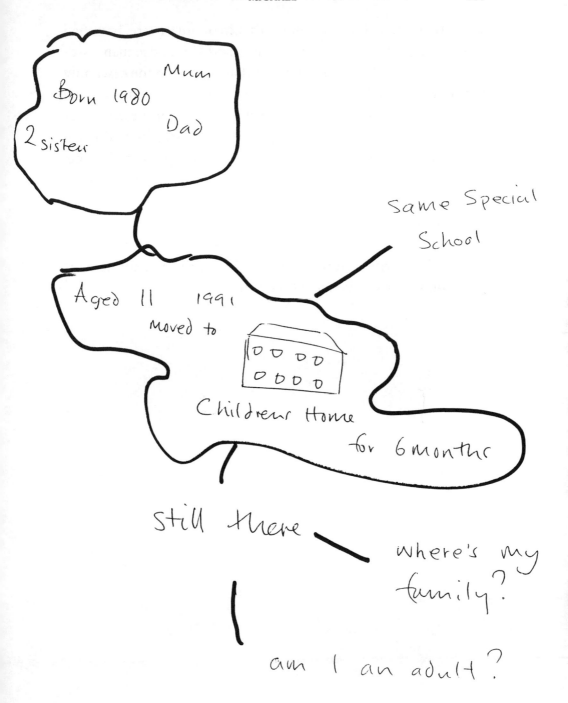

Figure 14.1 Lifemap – Michael

who have no learning disability, either in or out of care, have had some experience of decision making and the consequences of that process. For Michael, this has not always been the case: only now at the age of 17 is he getting more of a chance to make small decisions for himself, such as choosing what food he wants, or making himself a drink. In being allowed this freedom, Michael is being encouraged to demonstrate skills appropriate to his age. Nevertheless, when it comes to bigger issues such as where he is to live and who he is to spend his time with, he continues to have no choice in the matter.

By being allowed choice in such a limited range of areas, is Michael still suffering a form of oppression? Are the choices he is being allowed to make mere tokenism?

15

Adam

Adam was born in January 1985 in a large town in the West Country. His birth took place in hospital, and, although there had been no signs that there were going to be any complications, it proved to be traumatic. The circumstances surrounding these complications were described by Adam and his parents, who have suggested that the midwife who was looking after the birth made a mistake. His parents told me that if the blood pressure of a mother falls beneath a certain level, then a doctor must be informed and an emergency caesarean carried out. In Adam's case, although his mother's blood pressure did fall below this point on several occasions, the necessary precautions were not taken for some six hours, by which time it was too late and any damage had already happened.

After this, Adam had to spend 13 days in the hospital's special care baby unit. The issues surrounding his birth were explained to him at a very early stage, as it was felt important for him to know what had happened. Adam understands very clearly what went wrong, and feels 'very cross' and 'frustrated' at the situation, in that it could have been prevented. He does, however, find a humorous side to his birth, joking that he was born on the wrong day: he was born at 1am on the 12th, but, had there been no complications, he would have been born on the 11th.

When Adam was 19 months old, he went to a well-known clinic within an east European country, which practised what is known as 'conductive education'. He stayed there for five or six

years, along with members of his family. He does not have many
clear memories of this time, or of the processes of conductive
education and the exercises that he had to do. However, he does
remember his final year there, which he found boring because he
had reached a point beyond which the staff could not take him.
He also has clear memories of the food! He spent a long time
during our discussion talking about the food and asking his
mother if she knew how to make the various dishes he had at this
school. He had forgotten about this aspect of his early life, and it
was pleasing that our discussion had stirred these happy
memories. Adam took great delight in trying to remind his
mother of a dish that consisted of 'grey ball things' because he
really liked these. All of his good memories were of food, but he
did have a few bad memories too, including feelings of boredom
and also of 'horrible medicine' that he had to take: even his
parents were not sure what this medicine was for. Adam also
talked about a grumpy laundry man who did not like foreigners!

When he returned from Eastern Europe, Adam started at a special school that followed a similar programme to the one in which
he had been participating over the previous few years. However,
this school was in Sussex, and Adam's family were living in the
West Country. This meant that he had to board for five days a
week, spending the weekend at home with his family. This
proved to be difficult for all of them, because his parents would
pick him up on a Friday evening and drive him home, meaning
that it would be bed time before they reached home and they
would then have to drive back on Sunday, leaving no quality time
as a family. The arrangement lasted only two years before Adam
left the school 1992.

In 1994 Adam started at another special school in the eastern
area of Hampshire. When he first started he did enjoy it, but over
time he said that he started to dislike it more and more. This was a
result of Adam joining the Scouts and beginning to appreciate
that, compared with his new friends, he was missing out on a

great many opportunities, and that the education that he was receiving was far too slow for his abilities. He saw that he was being held back within the special school. He states quite definitely that he 'does not like being in special education' and made reference to the song 'Brick in the Wall' by Pink Floyd, which begins 'We don't need no education'.

Adam recognises the injustice of the system, and has in the past written letters to the head of his school. He is planning to do so again, his most recent complaint being concerned with the SNA (Special Needs Assistance) assistance that he should be receiving. His LEA (Local Education Authority) funding includes the provision of a personal SNA: however, this funding is used to pay for assistance for the whole class and not just for him. He receives this extra help on only one Thursday out of ten. As this school is not meeting his needs, he is due to start at a mainstream secondary school in September this year and, as part of the preparation and transition for this move, he has been attending the new school for a few days over the past few months in order to get used to it. When asked directly how he felt about these visits, he replied 'it's all right', but the impression I received was that he was looking forward to going to the new school.

The whole of Adam's change in attitude has come about from his joining the Scouts, where he has made new friends who attend mainstream schools, and he has therefore seen that there is a whole different world that he wants to be a part of. He joins in all of the activities that his pack does and has built up good friendships with some of the other boys, to an extent that they go to each other's houses, something he had not experienced before. He used to find it frustrating that his two younger sisters would bring their friends home to play, but he did not have a chance to do this. He is now hoping that this opportunity will increase when he starts at the local school, so that he can make lots of local friends. As his Scout pack is out of town he is reliant on others to get him to his friends, but, if he makes new friends who lives near to him, Adam hopes he will not need these lifts.

Adam has just started to use a communication aid called a Lightwriter. This will, it is hoped, eventually enable him to communicate more easily at his new school. At the present time, however, he finds it frustratingly slow because he has not yet mastered it properly. He wants it to work straightaway and, like most boys of his age, finds it difficult to see that practice makes perfect.

Adam does understand the limitations that his disability causes. For example, he told me that he would like a Safari Land Rover, but he knows that this will be difficult because of his impairment. He also believes strongly that some restrictions are not of his making, but a problem of society and the perceptions of other people. Again, although he can make a joke of an incident if someone is very patronising to him, such behaviour does make him frustrated.

16

Conclusion
Reading the Maps and Stories

We want to draw this volume to a close by reflecting on how the process of lifemapping may be used.

An example of one possible use occurred just as this book was going to press, and the 1998 *Community Care* awards for excellence and innovation in social care were announced (see Thompson 1998). The Voluntary Sector Innovation Award went to The Sharing Caring Project managed by Sheffield Mencap, a project which involves the production of some four hundred Life Books. These are to be used so that older carers of people with learning difficulties can pass on their knowledge and expertise to others who may be taking on some of the caring roles. It is clear that the inclusion of a lifemap in each such book would be one way of communicating a lot of useful information in an attractive and effective way.

Another instance is the use of the lifemap to make information accessible. One of the more noticeable factors about professionals of all kinds is that they have two distinct kinds of language: one for use with colleagues in the same profession, and another for use in talking to their non-professional friends. Both kinds of language convey information, but the former tends to be somewhat closed and exclusive, whereas the latter can be accessed far more widely. Life stories should fit into the category of being accessible to many people, but too often, carers of people with learning difficulties, who have not been provided with opportunities to learn the professional jargon (and may not wish to have such an opportunity), find it difficult to convey information about the people for whom they are caring. Again life stories may fulfil this role. However, merely to read life stories or a lifemap can never be a substitute for really getting to know the person.

A third possible use lies in the use of lifemaps in the process of assessment. We are familiar with the fact that it is a common experience of people with learning difficulties that they are 'assessed' periodically throughout their lives, and indeed the life stories contained in this book refer to this process specifically in the cases of Peter, Matthew and Mat. Outside of the field of medicine, health and social services, most of us encounter the concept of assessment in a more general sense, in education or in career development, and it may be worth comparing these different implications of this same term.

For most of us, an assessment is part of a continuing learning process, which can be life long. In an ideal model, assessment is part of a feedback system which informs us of our progress and establishes what our next set of targets ought to be. In the more specialised sense of assessment, in the fields of medicine, health and social services, it is possible for this same ideal model of feedback to operate. In the case of lifemapping, feedback and the building upon that feedback is crucial if the exercise is to work to its fullest extent. What happens in lifemapping is that the interviewers attempt, on the basis of what they are told, to draw out the significant events in the lives of other people. Because of its pictorial nature, the lifemap is capable of detailed assessment without requiring high-level reading skills. It can, therefore, be used to chart an agenda for the establishment of targets and goals. These may be couched in specific terms of tasks, or more generally in terms of emotional change. Thus, there is no reason why interviewers should not revisit the lifemaps to examine whether the interviewees still see the overall pattern of their lives in the same terms which they did when they first drew the map.

These lifemaps can, however, have a more general use for all members of society. Robert Atkinson (1998) points out that life stories have served four classic functions: bringing us more into accord with ourselves, with others, with the mystery of life, and with the universe around us. These are, we suggest, universal human interests, and there is no reason why a lifemap could not form the basis of exercises designed to meet some of these functions. The lifemaps and stories will always be the property of the storyteller, and they will be in the unique position of being the only people who know the most up-to-date version. There is a sense in which we all need continually to validate our life stories with the images we have of ourselves. Similarly, our life story changes in emphasis and interpretation through comparison with those of others, and this, in turn, may help in the quest to understand more about the mystery of life. Just how we fit into the larger picture of the universe has occupied the minds of philosophers since the beginning of time. If no other purpose is served, at least our life story will provide more data for analysis on the road to discovering answers to this great mystery.

The power of the life story with regard to all these aspects has recently been exemplified by the experience of a friend of Barry's. She very recently lost her father and after his death she was told that he was not her real father. Her mother told her that her real father was an American serviceman from North Carolina who had been stationed in England during the Second World War. So, suddenly, her whole life, and the meanings she had constructed from it, were totally transformed. The people she had known as brother and sister and grandmother were no different, but her sense of their relationship with her was changed. She is trying hard to reconstruct the story, although she is, as yet, undecided as to how much she wants to discover. One thing is clear, however; she has a need to make sense of it all, to own again a coherent story that fits the person she now finds herself to be. It may be that constructing a lifemap would help in this process, just as it might help those who find the need to rediscover a sense of their identity following a divorce.

Collecting the lifemaps

On pages 13–19 we outlined some of the ways in which our students collected the life stories and developed the lifemaps. They reported that they felt more comfortable about the exercise when they were gathering material from a person whom they had known for some time. Although we described different methods of collecting the stories, we did not prescribe one particular method to be used. Just as a life story and lifemap is unique, so are the circumstances and situations in which one person will meet another to share information. Nevertheless, there are some general rules which can be applied to the tasks of collecting the stories and drawing the maps:

1. regularly check the person has given informed consent and understands what will happen to the material

2. involve the storyteller in all aspects of the process of storytelling, including the analysis

3. show the person samples of lifemaps, including your own, so he or she can choose a particular and personal style of representation

4. wherever possible, and always with persmission, record the session in which the life story is told

5. try to have a range of media available for recording the life story: e.g. audio tape-recorder, video tape-recorder, different sizes of paper, coloured pens, still camera, etc.

6. always go back and check your early drafts and your final version of the life story with the storyteller

7. allow sufficient time (at least an hour) if you are collecting a life story in one session

8. let the storyteller choose where you collect the story and try to ensure there are no distractions, especially from other people who may want to correct or prompt the storyteller

9. the life story and lifemap belong to the storytellers – encourage them to use these resources in a creative way

10. lifemaps are best drawn on large sheets on a large flat surface.

Range of analytical frameworks

There is a sense in which by allowing publication of their stories, the storytellers are accepting that they become public property. This means, among other things, that the stories are available for others to analyse. These, and other published stories, will already have at least two levels of analysis applied to them. The first is controlled by the storyteller in so much as they choose what they are going to disclose and in what form. The second is applied by the student or researcher in interpreting the story. The first level includes analysis of how things felt, and we have probably all experienced the way in which events in our lives may be relayed in different ways depending upon the person to whom we are telling the story. A mother may well describe her relationship with her child in quite different ways when talking to her husband and when talking to a friend. In the second level, researchers may place emphasis on particular aspects of what they hear because of their own attitudes, beliefs, experiences and knowledge. They may choose to write one part of a story because it fits with their prejudice, or leave out another part because they find it difficult to listen to, or because they cannot believe it to be true. However, all the final versions published in this volume have been checked by the storytellers and can, therefore, be claimed to be legitimate subjects for analysis.

One of the benefits of publishing life stories is the provision of data which can be analysed in a range of different ways. There are, for example, certain established methodologies for coming to an understanding of the experiences of the learning disabled. Jean Vanier's framework (cited by Wolfensberger 1987) describes the typical 'wounds' of disabled people according to the following sixteen categories:

1. being a burden to loved ones

2. having a real impairment

3. involuntarily material poverty

4. having a functional impairment

5. being relegated to low status

6. being rejected, perhaps by family, neighbours, community, society, professionals

7. 'putting away' via segregation and congregation

8. discontinuity with the physical environment

9. social and relationship discontinuity

10. personal insecurity, perhaps even dislike of oneself

11. loss of control, perhaps of rights and freedom

12. impoverishment of experience

13. having one's life wasted

14. being suspected of multiple deviancy

15. symbolic 'marking' and 'funny imaging'

16. being brutalised.

Wolfensberger (1972), on the other hand, provides a taxonomy based on the premise of eight social roles ascribed to devalued groups, including people with learning difficulties, and these could be used as a matrix for the analysis of the stories in this book. The roles are:

1. as a subhuman organism

2. as an object of dread

3. as an eternal child

4. as a menace

5. as a sick organism

6. as an object of pity

7. as a holy innocent

8. as an object of ridicule.

The students who collected the life stories used them to demonstrate their own understanding of different frameworks for ethical and equal opportunities issues. We have not, however, pursued this particular form of analysis, but have chosen instead to draw attention to certain common themes within the stories which may provide the reader with a greater sense of 'getting to know' the people whose lives have been described.

It is perhaps unsurprising that there is one set of themes in the stories which highlights the similarities between these individuals and all other members of society, and another which foregrounds their sense of difference. The former set includes:

○ a sense of pride in the family and its importance

○ valuing special, permanent relationships

○ wanting to be listened to

Whilst the latter reads as follows:

○ not being able to choose who you live with

○ being treated as 'different'

- ◦ not knowing why things are happening to you
- ◦ not having money
- ◦ wasting time
- ◦ not feeling in control.

Feeling the same
A sense of pride in the family and its importance

There is a sense in which the people whose lives are recorded within this book may have an unusually intense relationship with members of their families. In the introduction, we referred to the implications of that word 'visit' which occurs so often within these stories, suggesting that this implied transitory and impermanent relationships. It is almost certainly the case that the people described here will have become accustomed to periods of intense interest from others who are not members of their families: social workers, health care workers and a range of other professionals. However, these periods of intense interest will, in many cases, have been very brief and may often have been terminated without any degree of sensitivity. We are well aware that our own interest, and that of our students, falls within this same category.

In that context, the stability and permanence of family relationships assumes a much greater significance than it would for most members of society. Most of us have some degree of choice in beginning, maintaining, continuing or terminating non-family relationships: for the people in this book that is yet another choice which they have not been given.

Even the very process of the collection of these stories demonstrates both the strength of family relationships and its unique character. Mat's story, for example, could not have been told in any detail without the intervention of his parents, who supplied detail and clarification. Few members of society are so dependent on others to provide the narrative of their own histories: this is a dependence we would usually expect to find only in the very young or the very old. In some of the stories told here, there is a real danger that the person described will lose that sense of individual personal history when the parents are no longer there to help in the telling of the narrative.

For all of us, our identities are framed and supported by memories which can be shared with others: indeed it is the very act of mutually agreeing what memories are important to us and how we view them that forms the basis of many of our closest relationships. Two examples from fictional works may serve to illustrate this point.

In Eric Chappell's play *Theft* (1996), John and Trevor have known each other since they were at school. However, one of the turning points of the play is the comparison between their memories of school days: in Trevor's mind, he protected the younger John from bullies, but John remembers Trevor as bully-in-chief, trapping his fingers in a desk on one occasion and breaking his arm on another. Trevor has no memory of these incidents.

In the film *Smooth Talk* (1985), directed by Joyce Chopra, one of the most poignant scenes between the two sisters who are at the centre of the piece comes when Connie, the younger girl, describes to her sister, June, a childhood memory. She talks of a time when she had been really cold from playing in the snow and her frozen hands had been warmed back to life by the tender love of June. The lyricism of this scene is brutally shattered as June replies that she has no memory of this time at all.

We are all dependent upon that set of memories which are shared with those whom we love, and which have an agreed significance for all parties involved. With that context in mind, it is not difficult to see how and why, in the lives recorded in this book, blood is demonstrably thicker than water.

Mary, for example (p.32), 'longed to be like her sisters'. She appears, in fact, to be constructing her identity from the mirror image of her twin sister, and she remains confused as to why they should have been treated so differently for what was, in essence, the same behaviour. Despite a period of time during which family contact was infrequent, Mary represents the big adventures in her life as those like her trip to America, which involve keeping in touch with her brothers, sisters, nephews and nieces.

Margaret, despite suffering abuse from her father and finding that some relatives did not wish to have anything to do with her, still shows a keen interest in family. She continues to visit the graves of her grandmother and grand/father, and visits her own mother.

Peter's parents lived apart and, as his life developed, he seemed increasingly to lose his independence. However, he has fond memories of living with his mother when he was 17, and also talks happily of a short stay with his aunt.

At first glance, Len's life seems more concerned with institutions and routines than with family, but we learn that, during the really difficult time (see p.51, 'I don't know how I survived it in there') it was his mother and brother who got him through.

For Lisa, family links with the navy seem to be of particular importance: not only did these links determine where she was brought up, they also provided her with a sense of pride. From the time when her mother died, while Lisa was quite young, Lisa saw herself as an important member of the family. She 'started doing all the things in the house and had to "look after" her Dad' (p.56). After her sister had moved away from the family home, Lisa 'had to do everything then' (p.57).

Madge's family remained in touch while she was at a hospital boarding school, and she was 'very happy to be back home' (p.63). Her brothers' weddings feature high in her memories, as does her father's death. Whilst she is now living more independently, Madge expresses a fond concern for her mother and keeps in regular contact. Her biggest adventure (going to Australia) was undertaken with her mother.

Tim, we are told, 'is filled with a sense of visible pride, and his face lights up' (p.71) when he is talking about his sister and niece. He 'greatly admires' (p.71) one of his two brothers and clearly loves their regular contact. He also seems proud of where he was born as he tries to encourage people to visit the village.

For Sue it 'was very hard for her' (p.83) when her parents moved away back to Scotland.

Jane shares her vivid memory of the death of her nan: 'I used to visit Nan a lot but she's dead now ... I was sad, I still miss her sometimes' (p.88). She maintains regular contact with her large number of brothers and sisters, and once again, her main adventures (visiting California) are directly concerned with her immediate family.

Mat's story relies heavily upon his parents for detail, and it would seem that, at 24 years of age, he still is very dependent on his mother and father.

Michael left his family home at the age of 11 and has remained away for six years. He still visits the family once a month and other people seem to see creating a family-type home for him as a priority – 'staff say he needed to feel secure' (p.107), and 'he needed to belong' (p.108). The staff tried to find a foster home for Michael and continued to try and get him returned to the family home.

Adam is still of an age where you would expect his family to be a central and important part of his life. He clearly has a very supportive family who have listened to him and helped him express his desires and opinions.

Valuing a special relationship

As indicated earlier, most of the life stories highlight how special and important the relationships within the immediate family can be in giving people a sense of history and belonging. In addition, most of us develop special relationships outside the family circle and these often become 'best friends' or partners. The value of such a relationship is another theme that runs through many of the life stories.

Mary met Albert late in her life, but it is clear from her story just how special he is to her: 'I was the last one to get married, I always wanted to get married' (p.32).

Peter recalls how he used to go out with his best friend, David, when they lived with a number of house-mates. Although Peter did not really like living there, he fondly remembers his friend (p.46).

Lisa is living with one of her friends that she made at school and two other close friends: 'Lisa says that she "loves it"!' (p.60).

Tim has never had a girlfriend but would like one 'very much' (p.74).

Colin particularly values the time he spends with his co-workers and the trips to the football matches with J. (p.79).

Jane fondly remembers her best friend Mary and has many photographs of their time together (p.87). She still sees her friends from Wales twice a year and keeps in regular contact through letters and the telephone (p.89).

Adam is looking forward to making local friends from the school nearby. He has made friends at the Scouts and wants special friends like his sisters have (p.115).

Wanting to be listened to

It is a truism nowadays that some voices are listened to more often than others. It is only within the second half of the twentieth century that women have found their voices heard and their views respected: before then, the female voice on committees and in decision making was frequently dismissed. Many people whose life stories are told here have found that their voices remain unheard.

Mary, for example, wanted to be listened to when she was trying to understand why she was being separated from her twin sister (p.30). She also wanted to be listened to when she told the police about having her money stolen (p.34).

Peter must feel as though no one is listening to him as, 'every time he asks someone what is happening he is told that he will be assessed again soon. This has been going on for almost a year' (p.48).

When Len wanted to move to a different ward no one listened (p.52): he feels 'if he did not like something, he ought to be allowed to say so' (p.52).

Perhaps Sue's description of herself – 'I cannot communicate with people' (p.83) – was rooted in the fact that people did not listen. The student who listened to her story felt Sue was a good communicator.

Matthew enjoys his time at the 'consumer-led' day service, and one reason is because people at the service are 'more mature, they talk to me sensibly and give me sensible ideas' (p.103). It could also mean that he is now being listened to.

There is a sense within the stories that the participants feel that they are listened to now, as opposed to the settings they were in previously. This may reflect improving services where people with learning difficulties are beginning to be listened to. It may also reflect the fact that the storytellers are more likely to participate if they are experiencing a period when they feel they are being heard. There may still be many people in our communities who are not being heard.

Feeling different

Choosing who you live with

The life maps of Barry and Geoff (pp.26–27) show that they left their respective family homes either as older teenagers or as young 20-year-olds. This represents a pattern that is common within their culture. They also began to actively choose the people with whom they lived. This pattern is the exception amongst the people whose stories are related in this book.

Mary left home at 16 and, for nearly 50 years, had no choice about who she lived with. At 64 she was finally allowed to make a choice and to marry the person she wanted to live with.

Margaret left home even earlier. She was only 13 and still she does not know why she had to leave. Although she likes it better where she is living now, she has had no choice in her 60s as to who she lives with.

Peter lived at home until his mother died. He still has had no choice with regard to live-in partners and we are told that one person he lives with 'caused a great deal of trouble, so much so, indeed, that Peter asked if he could be moved to another house'. He is nearly 60 years old.

Len did leave the family home at the age of 22, but this was to go to a hospital where he remained until he was in his 40s. He has now moved to a home in the community where he was able to choose some decorations and furniture, but not the people he lives with. He feels the other men in the home do not like him – 'they are their own worst enemies, wanting each other dead' (p.54). He says they have now got used to one another, but there is no love lost between them.

Lisa stayed at home until she was 40 and then went to live with her sister, even though she wanted to live on her own. Six years ago she moved to live with friends and is now very happy.

Madge spent some of her childhood in hospitals but stayed at home until she was 43. She did not choose who she now lives with but feels more independent and is looking forward to the future.

It is not clear when Tim left the family home, but, at the age of 42, it is evident that he has never had any say in whom he lives with.

Colin moved from the family home at 16 but was in his early 30s before he moved into a small group home. Again, he has had no choice about who shares the home with him.

Sue has had no opportunity to choose whom she lives with and she is at an age when Barry and Geoff were already parents.

Jane still lives with her family at the age of 33 as does Mat (25), Matthew (23), and, less surprisingly, Adam at 13. Michael, now 18, left home at the age of 11 and moved to an institution where he still remains. He has had no choice about whom he lives with.

Being treated differently.

We do not object to being treated differently to one another particularly if we see that difference as providing us with some advantage. We do not usually want to be treated exactly like every one else. We want our uniqueness to be recognised and taken into account. However, when we do not know why we are being dealt with in a different way, or if we perceive the different treatment as placing us in a disadvantageous situation, we usually complain. The life stories in this book contain many examples of individuals being treated differently from most other people in society (e.g. not being given choices, being paid very small amounts of money for work, going to different sorts of schools, etc.), and it may be the case that the people themselves do not always perceive these different treatments as being disadvantageous. However, there are examples where the person is clearly disturbed by these apparently different approaches and outcomes.

Mary 'could not see why her family had sent her away and not her sister who had also been 'meeting a young man' (p.30). At the age of 70, Mary still does not understand why she was sent away and none of her sisters were. 'They never been in the homes, that's what I can't understand. My sisters were as bad as me. They used to play up like hell but Dad wouldn't say anything to them, only to me. I was shut in and can't get over it really. Because why should I suffer and not the others?' (p.34).

Margaret was 'sent away' at the age of 13. Her childhood took on a quite different routine from then, and when she was much older, the very person who was in the trusted position of managing her home abused her.

Peter felt different as 'no one will play football with you when you only have one good arm', and he remembers that 'he used to read and write outside in the playground while the other children were inside' (p.44). What may be of significance is that it is not clear from Peter's story just what is wrong with his arm or when it was perceived to be a problem: this narrative seems to have been subsumed into the larger 'problem' of his learning difficulty.

Lisa recalls how the older children picked on her because she 'was different' and 'smaller than they were' (p.56). She was often left out of games, but she did not know why.

Madge was not allowed to walk to school like her brothers did. She did understand why her mother wouldn't let her walk to school, but Madge still felt it was unfair. She also feels angry about the way she was treated differently when her father was killed in a road accident – 'Someone could have told me earlier why I was waiting at the hospital' (p.65).

Tim, at the age of 42, lives where only other people are allowed in the kitchen of the home, and his future plans are devised by others when he is not present (p.73). He must also wonder why, at his age, he has never been to a football match, even though is one of his great interests.

Sue tells us, 'I hated going to the ESN schools because I was treated differently from school I went to before' (p.82).

Not knowing why things are happening to you

There are occasions when we may not want to know what is happening to us. These often related to some expected dreadful outcome when we either put our trust totally into someone else's hands, or, deny there is a problem. For example, some people would rather not know what the surgeon is going to do, and some try many different ways to forget that they are flying. One partner may deny the breakdown in communication as the relationship begins to fail. However, for most of the time we need to know why things are happening to us in the way they are. It gives a sense of meaning and purpose to our existence that helps reinforce and reshape our identities. For the people in our stories the same applies. They have a need to know what is happening, a need to make sense of the world. Over and over again there are examples of where this is not the case. Sometimes these instances involve what might be termed major life events (e.g. not knowing why you moved from one city or home to another), and others relate to what might be considered every day events (e.g. not knowing why you are doing the same task each day).

Mary still does not know why she was sent away from home, and Margaret does not know why she had to go to a convent. She 'did 24 years' (p.42) for stealing a sixpence. Margaret could also not understand why the manager of her home, 'came to my room at night, I didn't like what he did to me. Why did he always save me for Christmas?' (p.135).

Tim does not know why he can't make a phone call to his brother or sister when he wants to and he does not seem to know why he is unable to make affectionate relationships with women.

Michael wonders why he cannot go home and must feel confused about his family (p.109), and Adam had no idea why he was taking 'horrible medicine' (p.114).

Having money

At a very late stage in the writing of this book, one of us was talking to an undergraduate living away from home for the first time. She confided that one of her biggest fears was dealing with money: she did, however, recognise that coping with money was a key factor in her becoming a mature, independent adult.

It would seem that most of our storytellers have little money that they see as their own. For some of the individuals, their income from benefits, which may constitute a reasonable sum in themselves but which are handled by others, leaves the person with only a very small amount, if any, each week. Not very long ago, one of us was asked to work with 'a disruptive young lady who stole'. She was a smoker and yet was only allowed £2.00 per week (less than the price of a packet of cigarettes). She did not need any kind of behavioural intervention to 'cure' her disruptiveness, she needed to have access to more money. Once this was organised (she had sufficient funds available from her benefits), she no longer stole nor was seen as disruptive. We may choose to work fewer hours or have less responsibility and therefore be poorer; our storytellers seem to have had no choice in the matter.

Len was paid £2.00 a day in the industrial unit at the hospital. Even in the 1980s, this would have been considered as very poor pay. Lisa thought the only good things about the centre she attended was that she got 'a bit of money' and 'saw her friends' (p.57). She now has the job she wants but is allowed to earn only a certain amount before she loses money from her benefits.

When Madge worked at a centre we are told, 'even at the time, this was a ridiculously low rate of pay', and even though she saved, every time she wanted to buy something she had to ask her parents for money (p.63). Jane, we are told, very much enjoys the sheltered scheme she takes part in, 'not least because she is paid £2.00 per day for her work' (p.50).

Readers of these stories might like to consider the difference it seems to have made to people when they have started to handle their own money. Although this only happened in only a couple of cases, it does seem to have had a significant impact.

Wasting time

Not only do we like to know what is happening to us, we also like to feel that what we are doing is meaningful and has purpose.

Whilst we may enjoy 'doing nothing', it is only in the context of inactivity being different from what we normally engage in. Many of us like playing sport for relaxation or on holiday: for Ryan Giggs or Steffi Graf, sport is work, not relaxation, and they presumably relax in quite different ways. Feeling that you are doing nothing is pleasant only if you are accustomed to being busy and being valued for what you do: doing nothing soon becomes boring and this is reflected in the stories. All too often we find that the 'work' given to the storytellers is patently not valued and is designed solely to keep them occupied.

Lisa found her day service a waste of time 'doing boring work like taking stamps off envelopes' (p.57). Madge found the education classes at her new day service boring compared with the work she had previously undertaken (p.64). From Tim's story, it is difficult to identify any purposeful activities that he is involved in. He must feel he is wasting most of his time.

Has anything changed?

At the outset we wondered whether the stories would reveal that their tellers had different lives according to how long ago they were born: would the younger people have more opportunities? Clearly, the readers must make their own minds up on this question, but we would suggest that, sadly, little seems to have changed.

The sorts of factors which seem to us to have remained constant would include the concern on the part of the tellers of the stories that they were given attention only when they demonstrated 'bad' behaviour or underachievement; concern over the expression of their sexuality; or their spirituality; concern about being placed in noisy environments; a concern that their different concept of time was not respected – often the tellers of these stories seem not to have an accurate sense of chronology or dates, but they clearly treasure the security of a routine or ritual, certain activities on certain days, and this perspective is not always recognised by those working with them.

It may be best to accentuate one of the most positive ways in which those whose stories are told here are similar to many other members of society, and that is in their humour. Earlier we have expressed the view that much of the work given to the people in this book is either poorly paid or unfulfilling or both. We end with the views of Jane, however, who is adamant that, although she likes her job, she would not wish to be there every day!

Finally, let us return to the observation referred to above by Robert Atkinson that life stories serve the four classic functions of bringing us more into accord with ourselves, with others, with the mystery of life, and with the universe all around us. The stories in this collection, and the lifemaps which gave rise to those stories, demonstrate how precious it is to come into accord with ourselves and with our own sense of who we are. That process may often be denied to people with learning difficulties, who may find their narratives difficult to articulate. Lifemapping can liberate them and, indeed, can liberate any one of us.

References

Atkinson, D. (ed) (1993) *Past Times: Older People with Learning Difficulties Look Back on Their Lives.* Buckingham: Open University Press.

Atkinson, D. and Williams, F. (eds) (1990) *'Know Me As I Am': An Anthology of Prose, Poetry and Art by People With Learning Difficulties.* Kent: Hodder and Stoughton in Association with the Open University and MENCAP.

Atkinson, D., Jackson, M. and Walmsley, J. (1997) *Forgotten Lives.* Kidderminster: BILD.

Atkinson, R. (1998) *The Life Story Interview.* London: Sage.

Chappell, E. (1996) *Theft.* London: Samuel French.

Deacon, J. (1974) *Tongue Tied.* London: MENCAP.

Gillman, M., Swain, J. and Heyman, B. (1997) "Life history" or "case history". *Disability and Society*, 12, 675–94.

Goodley, D. (1996) 'Tales of hidden love'. *Disability and Society*, 11, 333–48.

Humphreys, S., Evans, G. and Todd, S. (eds) (1987) *Lifelines: An Account of the Life Experiences of Seven People With a Mental Handicap Who Used the NIMROD Service.* London: King's Fund Publishing.

Kinsella, W. P. (1984) *The Moccasin Telegraph and Other Stories.* London: Viking.

Kirkpatrick, K. and Earwaker, S. (1997) 'Turning words into actions'. *Community Living*, 10, 4, 20–21.

Miles, B. (1997) *Many Years From Now.* London: Secker and Warburg.

Radford, J. P. and Tipper, A. (1988) *Starcross: Out of the Mainstream.* Toronto: G. Allan Roeher Institute.

Ramcharan, P., Roberts, G., Grant, G. and Borland, J. (eds) (1997) *Empowerment in Everyday Life: Learning Disability.* London: Jessica Kingsley Publishers.

Ryan, J. and Thomas, F. (1995) *The Politics of Mental Handicap.* Harmondsworth: Penguin.

Stalker, K. (1998) 'Some ethical and methodological issues in research with people with learning difficulties'. *Disability and Society*, 13, 1, 5–19.

Swain, J., Heyman, B. and Gillman, M. (1998) 'Public research, private concerns: ethical issues in the use of open-ended interviews with people who have learning difficulties'. *Disability and Society,* 1, 1, 21–36.

Thompson, A. (1998) 'Reaching for the best'. *Community Care,* December, 26–7.

Usher, J. (1993) *Life Story Work: A Therapeutic Tool for Social Work.* Social Work Monographs: Norwich UEA.

West, C. (1990) 'The new cultural politics of difference' In R. Ferguson (ed) *Out There.* Cambridge, Mass: MIT Press.

White, M. and Epston, D. (1990) *Narrative Means to Therapeutic Ends.* New York: Norton.

Wildey, E. (1985) *My Life Story.* London: SITE at the City Lit.

Wolfensberger, W. (1972) *Normalisation: The Principle of Normalisation in Human Services.* Toronto:NIMR.

Wolfensberger, W. (1987) *The New Genocide of Handicapped and Afflicted People.* Syracuse University.

Further reading

Angrosino, M. V. (1998) *Opportunity House: Ethnographic Stories of Mental Retardation.* London: Sage.

Cumberbatch, G. and Negrine, R. (1992) *Images of Disability on Television.* London: Routledge.

Morris, J. (1991) *Pride Against Prejudice.* London: Women's Press.

Positive Tales. (1996) Milton Keynes: Living Archive Press.